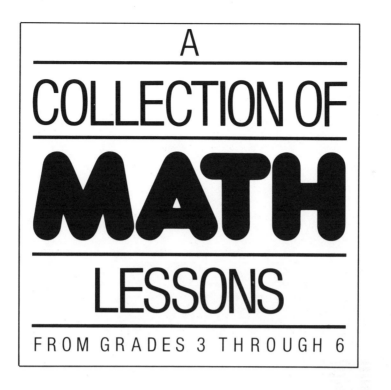

A
COLLECTION OF
MATH
LESSONS
FROM GRADES 3 THROUGH 6

A COLLECTION OF MATH LESSONS

FROM GRADES 3 THROUGH 6

BY MARILYN BURNS

MATH SOLUTIONS PUBLICATIONS

Art Direction and Design: Leslie Bauman and Molly Heron
Editing: Barbara Youngblood
Illustration: Martha Weston

Printed in the United States of America

ISBN 0-941355-00-4

Distributed by Cuisenaire Company of America, Inc.
P.O. Box 5026
White Plains, New York 10602-5026

Available on Videotape

Some lessons from each book in the series, *A Collection of Math Lessons,* have been
captured on three series of videotapes — *Mathematics with Manipulatives* (K-6),
Mathematics: Teaching for Understanding (K–6), and *Mathematics for Middle School* (6-8).
Classes of elementary and middle school students are taught by Marilyn Burns and other
instructors of Math Solutions.

The videotapes are available from Cuisenaire Company of America, Inc., P.O.Box 5026,
White Plains, NY 10602-5026. For information, telephone (800) 237-3142.

ACKNOWLEDGEMENTS

Special thanks to the teachers and children in whose classes the lessons were taught.

Dinah Chancellor, Bryan Independent School District, Texas
Sue Hill, Bellevue Public Schools, Washington
Sandra Nye, West Babylon Public Schools, New York
Gena St. Augustine, Mill Valley Public Schools, California
Anne Schaefer, Scarsdale Public Schools, New York
Stephanie Sheffield, Aldine Independent School District, Texas
Dee Uyeda, Mill Valley Public Schools, California
Jane Van Ryn, Bellevue Public Schools, Washington

CONTENTS

INTRODUCTION

I remember what daily math lessons were like when I was an elementary-school student. The teacher usually taught us by explaining and giving chalkboard demonstrations. We students were called upon to respond to questions, then given the chance to try problems at our seats. Sometimes we were sent to the board to do exercises. That was exciting because it was a treat to be allowed to write on the chalkboard, but scary because all the others saw when you made a mistake. Homework was often assigned; then we were on our own or had to call on our parents to help. Thus, we progressed through the math book.

Most of what was taught was arithmetic, and I remember the myriad rules and procedures I mastered. I learned to keep my columns neat, carry when adding, borrow when subtracting, add a zero in the second line when multiplying, bring down when dividing, add across the tops but not the bottoms with fractions, multiply across both the tops and bottoms when multiplying fractions, turn one fraction upside-down when dividing, and always reduce all fractions to lowest terms.

We also did word problems, for which we had to show our work and label our answers. I don't think we were very good at labeling answers, because we received constant reminders from teachers to do that. At all times we were expected to check our work. I don't think we were very good at that either, as teachers also reminded us to do that a great deal of the time.

I liked math. I liked the orderliness of arithmetic procedures. The rules made sense to me. They seemed useful. I took pleasure in doing neat papers. It wasn't so much that math was exciting to me as it was satisfying.

As a teacher, however, I learned that there definitely are the "haves" and "have-nots" among math students. For too many of my students, there was no appreciation of the orderliness in arithmetic procedures. They did not see rules as I did — as understandable, clever ways to arrive at correct answers. Instead, they saw them as a collection of mysterious methods to be memorized much as one would memorize nonsense rhymes.

After I'd given what I considered to be the clearest of explanations, it was not unusual for students to say, "If you'll just tell me what to do, I'll do it." Those students experienced no pleasure in facing a page of examples to copy and work; rather they felt hopelessness. Their papers were smudged, their columns never quite straight enough. As a new teacher, my suggestions for helping and encouraging my students were limited. "Think harder." "Can you remember how we did it yesterday?" "Just do this and you'll see." It wasn't that I was sure those suggestions would help. I just didn't know what else to do. My experience of having been one of the lucky ones in math was no help, and I worried that many of my students seemed not to be so fortunate.

It was hard to ignore the evidence that my approach to teaching math was uninspired. No matter how careful I was in preparing lessons or how earnest I was in presenting them, too many students were unmotivated. I knew that many found math boring. Neither they nor I were experiencing success or satisfaction.

The math lessons described in this book are very different from those I experienced as a child in elementary school and from those I taught as a beginning teacher. These lessons are the result of my reading, studying, attending workshops, trying activities in classrooms, talking with colleagues. They are examples of what I've come to believe makes good math teaching.

In these lessons I wanted students to feel that learning mathematics was not only for those who are lucky enough to catch on quickly, but also for all children. I wanted children to see mathematics as a subject that can spark wonder and curiosity. I wanted them to experience mathematics in areas other than arithmetic. And I wanted to teach lessons in which the children not only took delight in their learning, but also in which I took delight in my teaching.

I used five guiding principles in planning for the lessons I've described.

1. Each lesson was to be a problem-solving experience for the students. By that I mean that the children were given something interesting to ponder, something that required they think and reason.

2. The lessons would deal with important mathematics concepts so that children had the opportunity to develop and extend their understanding of mathematics.

3. As often as possible in lessons, children were given the chance to talk with me and with each other about what they were thinking and to describe their thoughts in writing.

4. Whenever appropriate to the lesson, children were given physical materials to use to help make math concepts real, to give them a way to verify their thinking, to help them approach math from a concrete rather than from an abstract perspective.

5. Classes were organized into small groups that worked together cooperatively to maximize children's opportunities to verbalize their thoughts, clarify their ideas, get reactions from others, and listen to others' points of view.

Years of experience and detailed planning went into each of these lessons. Most of them I've taught before, several times — to different classes, at different grade levels, and in different years. I've therefore had the chance to tinker with them. Friends have also tried them, and we've had the chance to compare results.

Though the lessons deal with a variety of topics and have been taught at a variety of grade levels, it is the similarity among them that convinced me to include these particular ones in this collection. They involved children in solving mathematical problems. They engaged children in thinking and talking about mathematical ideas. They drew mathematical insights from the children that were often fresh and original, and always a delight. The children were involved, interested, animated. In general these lessons represent a sampling of my teaching victories.

The lessons are written as vignettes. Each vignette begins with an introduction that explains the purpose of the lesson, describes the concepts being taught, and gives a rationale for the particular approach taken. The lessons vary in length. Some take place in a one-day teaching period; others span several days or a week.

In order to show how different students responded to the lessons, children's writing has not been edited. The presentation of the children's efforts is faithful to their actual work and includes their misspellings and grammatical errors. Some of the children's work has been photographed to illustrate their actual recordings.

Some of the lessons focus on standard topics, such as multiplication, word problems, and fractions, which usually receive the major share of attention in the elementary math curriculum. Other lessons focus on topics that traditionally receive less attention, from the strands of geometry, measurement, probability, and statistics. However, in most of the lessons, concepts from more than one area of mathematics are interwoven so that students have the opportunity to see the interrelatedness of mathematical ideas.

There were, of course, the usual mishaps and disruptions. A fire drill; a special band rehearsal; announcements over the loudspeaker; and a bloody nose, stomach ache, and playground casualty. These interferences are not included in the vignettes.

Also, behavioral problems cropped up. They are not included either. I chose not to refer to difficulties that were not related to the specific math goal. The behavioral problems encountered, however, were similar to those I've faced over the years.

Sara, one of the third graders, had great difficulty working coopera- tively and was a constant problem for her group members. Typical com- plaints were that Sara was being "too bossy" or "wasn't letting others take a turn." The group with Sara needed much more help than the others.

Brad, a third grader, was always in motion. He would get excited for all the right reasons and express his excitement in all the wrong ways. Brad needed help in focusing, and he often needed to have his energy quieted.

Mike, a sixth grader, was difficult to engage. During the palindrome les- son, I noticed that the other three members of his group were working away while he sat with his arms folded. I had to tell them that their behavior was not acceptable and negotiate with them to find a way for Mike to con- tribute. It worked, for that time at least. During another class, however, I found Mike at the sink playing with a plastic bag while his group was ex- ploring an activity.

In the midst of a lesson with the fifth graders, I overheard Brian say to Jerry, "Let's have a laughing contest." I was both amused and not amused. I approached Brian directly, "Why do you think that might be a good idea?" He was stumped for an answer. I posed another question, "What do you think might be a better idea for math class?" He and Jerry got to work.

Marcie, a fifth grader, had great difficulty working independently and with her group. She would continually come to me for help. Typically, as soon as the groups began to work, I'd see Marcie make her approach. Or sometimes I'd glance around while talking with a group, and there she would be. Marcie and I had many discussions about how I saw this prob- lem. She was a bright and capable child, and she improved, but she never did completely change her pattern.

These kinds of situations can develop in any classroom, whether the children are engaged in active math explorations or working from a text- book page, whether they are seated in desks in rows or working in coopera- tive groups. I try to deal with difficulties of these kinds by providing chil- dren with interesting problems to think about, concrete materials to work with, and as much encouragement as possible. When students are engaged both mentally and physically, behavioral problems seem to diminish.

SOME NOTES ABOUT THE MATHEMATICS
CHILDREN SHOULD BE LEARNING

Children who are taught to think mathematically can apply their mathematics understanding and skills to solve problems. They can see relationships and patterns and use numbers confidently to make decisions. Because they are mathematically secure, these children enjoy their mathematical explorations and are challenged and stimulated by them.

The lessons presented in this book were designed to help children become strong in their mathematical thinking. Powerful young mathematicians develop when mathematics is taught through a problem-solving approach: the goal is to help students make sense out of mathematics and to perceive its usefulness. The lessons structure experiences for children that help them learn mathematical concepts and see relationships among these concepts.

Traditionally, the major emphasis of the elementary mathematics curriculum has been on teaching children arithmetic — how to add, subtract, multiply, and divide whole numbers, fractions, decimals, and percents. What generally occurs in elementary classrooms is that children spend the bulk of their math time learning the arithmetic processes and practicing them with paper-and-pencil assignments.

Problem solving generally appears as an outgrowth of computation, with word-problem applications following the teaching and practice of each arithmetic skill. Though some attention is given to other topics in mathematics — geometry and measurement, most typically — they are taught in ways unrelated to the study of arithmetic and often are treated as optional or less important.

The teaching of mathematics at the elementary level must give substantial attention to concepts and skills from all strands — number, measurement, geometry, patterns and functions, statistics and probability, and logic. These strands are not separate and unrelated mathematical topics; they are arbitrary delineations that frequently overlap. Instruction in mathematics must incorporate concepts from all strands and emphasize the interrelatedness of the strands. Mathematical rules and procedures should not be taught in isolation, but in the context of problem-solving situations.

USING SMALL COOPERATIVE GROUPS

Students' learning is supported when they have opportunities to describe their own ideas, hear others explain their thoughts, speculate, question, and explore various approaches. Learning together in small groups gives students more opportunities to interact with concepts than class discussions do. Not only do students have the chance to speak more often, but also they may be more comfortable taking risks — trying out their thinking in problem-solving situations — in the setting of a small group.

Working in small cooperative groups maximizes the active participation of each student and reduces the isolation of individuals. A classroom that values and promotes social interaction provides children with support that is essential for learning. Working together was an integral part of the learning process in these classes.

When you place students into small groups, you must also reorganize the classroom physically, redefine the students' responsibilities, and consider the teacher's role in the class. For these lessons students were seated in groups of four whenever possible, with groups of three or five when necessary. All groups were heterogeneously formed, and students were reorganized regularly.

For several reasons it is valuable to have students work in heterogeneous groups that change from time to time. First of all, students' social skills improve as a result of their interaction with many different classmates. Also, working in heterogeneous groups is valuable for students of all ability levels: students slower to learn have the benefit of hearing ideas presented from several points of view; the opportunities for brighter students to verbalize their thoughts and justify their reasoning contribute to cementing and extending their understanding.

Getting students into groups of four is simple enough by having students move desks into small clusters of four each. To form the groups I randomly assign the students, using playing cards to do so. I label the clusters of desks – ace, 2, 3, 4, and so on – and take the corresponding cards from a deck. Groups are formed by shuffling the cards, distributing them, and asking all the aces to go to the ace group, and so forth. Chapter 8 describes a lesson in which the students were arranged for the first time by using this method.

The card method remixes students fairly well with each reshuffle and removes from the teacher the responsibility of deciding who works with whom. This is an advantage, especially in classrooms where boys feel unwilling to work with girls, or the opposite, or where cliques of students like to work together to the exclusion of others. Using cards handles these kinds of situations with the fairness of random selection.

Three rules are in operation when students are in groups of four:

1. Students are responsible for their own work and behavior.
2. Students must be willing to help any group member who asks.
3. Students may ask the teacher for help only when everyone in the group has the same question.

These rules must be explained to the class and discussed at least the first half dozen times the students work in groups; then they must be reinforced from time to time. The rules are useful only to the extent that they are understood and put into practice.

The first rule is not new for any student. Even so, it helps to clarify it with further explanations over time: "You have responsibilities in this class, and your job is to meet them. If you don't understand something, first ask your group for help." On the other hand: "If you do understand, don't take over and give answers. Listening to others' ideas is also a part of your individual responsibility." Also: "When there is an individual assignment, though you are sitting with your group, you will have your own work to complete. However, when your group has an assignment to complete jointly, your responsibility is to contribute to the group effort."

Two comments help to clarify the second rule: "Notice that the benefit of this rule is that you have three willing helpers at your side at all times, with no waiting for help." Also: "Remember that you are to give help when asked." Students may need to be reminded not to be pushy, to wait for group members to ask, and to help, not by merely giving answers, but by trying to find questions that would help someone focus on the problem at hand.

The third rule contributes greatly to the success of managing groups of four. It eliminates most of those procedural questions: "What are we supposed to do?" "When is this due?" "Can we take this home?" This rule directs students to seek help from each other first, relieving the teacher of the tedium of having to repeat directions or information over and over again.

Staying true to the third rule requires discipline on the part of the teacher. Teachers are used to responding directly to children and offering help whenever possible. When working with cooperative groups, teachers should ask students if they have checked with their groups, reminding them that only when all group members have the same question will assistance be given. Responding in this way may seem the opposite of responsive, sensitive, and helpful; however, it should be viewed as a way to help students learn to rely increasingly on themselves and each other so that they become more confident and independent learners.

The benefits of cooperative groups of four can be realized only when enough time and attention are given to implementing them in the classroom. There is nothing magical, no instant success, when seating students in groups of four and explaining the rules. The method takes practice, encouragement, and discussion before students learn to work together successfully. Though students have heard much about cooperation, functioning cooperatively is not a skill they have necessarily practiced. Though students have always been told that they are responsible for their own work and behavior, meeting that responsibility independently does not come naturally. And though teachers may intellectually accept the educational and social benefits of responding to students in cooperative groups rather than to individuals, they may need to change longstanding teaching habits.

THE ROLE OF THE TEACHER

It is important to consider the teacher's role in developing children's mathematical thinking and problem-solving abilities. Even in a classroom where there is an emphasis on student interaction, it is the teacher who directs the instruction, leads lessons, prompts responses, and paces the class.

In lessons, teachers need to emphasize the importance of working through problems, not merely getting correct answers. This means that errors must not be viewed as unfortunate mistakes, but as opportunities for learning. The teacher needs to make the classroom a safe place where new ideas can be tried out, so children feel free to risk making mistakes. Persistence in thinking, not speed, needs to be valued. Valuing quick, right answers does not help to establish a classroom environment that encourages the learning of mathematics.

Teachers need to urge students to find ways to verify their thinking for themselves rather than always relying on the teacher or on answer books. They should encourage students to explain their approaches and results, even when they are correct. Often teachers nod and affirm children's correct responses and question children only when they are wrong. Children catch on quickly when teachers question only incorrect responses.

It is important for teachers to remember that helping children develop understanding of mathematics concepts and skills cannot be a lesson objective, but must be considered a long-range goal. Time is often a concern for teachers. There is just a year to "get through" an enormous amount of material. Individual learning, however, does not happen on a time schedule and often requires more time than classroom instruction is organized to provide. Teachers must provide students with the time they need to learn. They must have the students push the curriculum rather than the other way around. They must not slip into teaching by telling for the sake of efficiency.

HOW TO USE THIS BOOK

The vignettes have been arranged in grade-level order, beginning with the lessons taught to third graders, continuing up to those conducted in sixth-grade classrooms. However, they may be read in any sequence. It is the cumulative effect derived from reading the collection that is important, not the specific sequence in which they are read.

The particular grade levels in which the lessons have been taught are not meant to imply that a lesson is suitable only for that grade level. Most are applicable to more than one grade level. Actually, it is beneficial for students to experience these sorts of activities more than once. Students come to activities they have encountered before with the benefit of previous experience and increased maturity.

Just as learning is enhanced in the classroom when students are given the opportunity to interact and exchange ideas, so will your understanding be supported through discussion with colleagues. You may find the following questions useful for reflection and discussion after reading one or several vignettes:

1. What concepts and skills were dealt with in the lesson?
2. How does your current textbook provide for instruction in this area?

3. Where would such a lesson fit in your math program?
4. How does the lesson promote students' problem-solving abilities?
5. What effect do you think the activities in the lesson can have on students' attitudes toward math?
6. How did the cooperative learning environment affect students' learning?
7. How could the lesson be improved?
8. How would you have responded differently in one or more instances?

PREPARING TO TEACH LESSONS

Each of these lessons required that I do two kinds of preparation. One was the thinking I had to do to plan out the lesson. The other was the gathering and organizing of the materials I needed. The preparation was costly in time, usually taking far more than the hour or so I would spend with the students. Even when I've taught a lesson before, making plans to teach it again for a different class always requires rethinking. I consider the needs, experience, skills, and personalities of the students. I reevaluate what happened the last time and try to make improvements.

Though the planning I did will be helpful to you when you get started, trying these lessons with your students will require that you consider how they will work with your students. Keep in mind that students in your classes will, of course, have responses that differ from those described in these particular situations. This is good, for comparing different responses can help you evaluate what occurs when you present the lessons.

The vignettes can help you picture how a teacher introduces a lesson, what the children actually do, how a teacher might respond – that is, what can be possible in a problem-solving math lesson.

As you read the vignettes, it is important to keep the objective of the instruction in mind. You should consider how this objective fits into children's mathematical learning and into your instructional program. Also, it is helpful to keep in mind that though the vignettes describe one path to the goal of the lesson, they describe only one path, certainly not the only path possible.

If a particular math activity is new to you, let the students know that. Learn with them. Present yourself to the class as an interested problem solver, an active learner willing to plunge into a new situation, even when you don't know what the answer or outcome will be. Model for your students an important attitude for a mathematics learner, that there is a difference between not knowing and not yet having found out. Most of all, enjoy the mathematics experiences with your children.

"I have eleven groups of 3. That makes 33 raisins, but my guess was 27."

C hildren in the third grade spend most of their mathematics instructional time on the arithmetic skills of addition and subtraction and beginning multiplication and division. Heavy emphasis is put on their mastery of those computational skills. Worksheet and textbook arithmetic drill predominate, with word problems as the main source for applying the skills. There is always a correct answer for the children's work; there is often only one correct way to reach that answer.

What is often missing for children in classroom instruction are experiences with numbers that reach beyond computation skills and word problems. Classroom instruction ought to provide this. Children need number experiences in which the main emphasis is on the thinking and reasoning needed to solve problems, rather than on demonstrating skills. Children need experiences where they use number skills and understandings in conjunction with other areas of mathematics, so they do not develop a narrow view of mathematics—that is, that mathematics is a collection of separate topics. Children need to confront numbers in ways that are less tidy than traditional paper-and-pencil practice, in ways that encourage them to estimate and make decisions where it isn't always possible to be exact. And children need these sorts of experiences regularly throughout the year.

This lesson models one such number experience. A class of third graders investigates small snack boxes of raisins in several problem-solving activities. During their investigations, the children apply whole number operations, estimate, consider statistical ideas, use measurements of volume and weight, and make proportional comparisons. The emphasis in the lesson is on the thinking the children bring to the problems. Throughout, the students are asked to explain their reasoning as they report their solutions.

Such a problem-solving lesson helps develop children's conceptual understanding of number operations. Several times during this lesson, teaching opportunities to focus on the operations emerged. When asked to group their raisins so it would be easy to see how many there were, the chance to discuss multiples was presented. When they were asked to share their raisins equally in their groups, the different methods reported led to a discussion of division. (One group chose a method that replicates what we normally do in the long division algorithm, though they had not yet had formal instruction on it.)

This lesson spanned one long class period of about an hour and a half. The children's attention did not lag. However, it was a great deal to cram into one session. An alternate plan, for presenting the lesson over two days, is described at the end of the chapter.

BEGINNING THE LESSON

In preparation for this lesson, I bought ½-ounce boxes (the smallest ones) of raisins, one for each student. I also bought 1½-ounce boxes of raisins, one box for each group of three or four students.

"Do you like raisins?" I asked the class. All but a few nodded assent. I showed them the small boxes I had brought and told them that each one of them would get to eat a box of raisins a bit later, if they wanted. "But first," I said, "we are going to do some mathematics with the raisins. I have several different activities for you to try, working together in your groups. For three of the activities, I will ask you to report your group's thinking in writing." Although I planned to give them specific directions for each activity when we did it, I told them this much now to prepare them for what I expected.

I held up one small box and asked them to think for a moment about how many raisins they thought might be in one of the small boxes. Many of the children were willing to make guesses. "12." "20." "50." "17." "40." "26." Nicholas, however, voiced a concern. "You can't tell," he said, "because raisins are different sizes, so there might be a different number in one box than in another." This did not deter the other children from continuing to guess, however, and soon all the children who were interested had had the chance to voice an opinion.

"You'll have the chance in a short while to find out how many raisins are in the small box," I continued. "Then we'll find out about Nicholas's thought that the boxes may contain different amounts. In just a moment I am going to give you each a box. Listen carefully to what I want you to do. You are to open the top of your box, but not to empty out the raisins. Instead, I want you to count the raisins you can see just by looking in from the top; then use that information to make an estimate about how many raisins you think are in the box.

"Don't touch or munch on any raisins yet — we'll get to that shortly. After you've examined your box, discuss your estimates in your groups and decide upon a group estimate of how many raisins are in a box. Your first writing task is to report this estimate, explaining your reasoning."

MAKING GROUP ESTIMATES

After giving each student a box, I circulated and listened as the children opened their boxes, peered inside and counted, and then talked in their groups to decide upon a group estimate. It was difficult for some to agree on a group estimate. Children got individually invested in their own estimates, and it took a good deal of prodding to focus them on coming to a group decision. When they had, I asked the groups to report their estimates and explain their reasoning.

Claire explained for her group: "We each counted how many raisins were on our top layer. Then we multiplied about four times. We each came out with an answer around 26. Twenty-six was decided to be our group estimate."

Trevor reported: "We think 30 raisins. When we looked in the box, we saw about 6 raisins, and we thought about five rows."

Two groups informally used averaging techniques to come to their estimates. Becky reported for her group, "Our group estimates 26 because Molly wanted 25 and Emilie and I wanted 27. So we took the inbetween number, which was 26."

The other group's individual estimates were more disparate. They agreed on a group estimate of 31. They explained their own estimates individually. Nicholas said, "I say 22 because I counted 11 on the top and timed it by 2." Ben said, "I think 42. I counted 7 levels and 6 on each level." Lucy explained her estimate of 27, "I counted 12 on top and figured there were 15 on the bottom." Nina explained her estimate and the group's decision, "I say 28 because I counted 11 on top and figured there was a little more than

15 on the bottom. Because 42 was our high and 22 was our low, we picked 31 because it is in the middle."

COUNTING AND SHARING THE RAISINS

The children's next tasks were to count the raisins in their boxes, then to figure out how many their group had altogether, and finally to divide the raisins equally. I gave the directions for each task separately.

I gave each student a sheet of paper, explaining they were to spill their raisins on the papers to count them. "When you count your raisins," I explained, "arrange them on the paper so that I can easily see how many you have. When you've all done this, I will record on the chalkboard how many raisins you each have."

While they were counting their raisins, I listed the numbers from 25 to 45 on the chalkboard. I planned to use tally marks to record their individual counts and then see what conclusions they could draw from the information.

Children arranged their raisins in different ways. I called on Dusty to report first. He announced, "I have 38 raisins."

I made a tally mark on the board next to the 38 and asked, "How did you group them?"

"I did it in 5s," Dusty answered, "but I had one group with only 3."

"How many full groups of 5 did you have?" I asked.

Dusty counted. "Seven groups."

"Let's count by 5s," I said to the class, "and see how Dusty got 38 raisins." I held up seven fingers, and we counted by 5s to 35 and added 3 more to get 38.

We continued around the room, each child reporting. I marked each count. We verified some, but not all, by counting the groups as we had done with Dusty.

Though grouping by 5s was a common response, children also used other ways to arrange their raisins. Hannah grouped by 3s and reported, "I have eleven groups of 3. That makes 33 raisins, but my guess was 27." Nina arranged hers into three groups of 10 with 6 left over. Ryan spread his raisins on his paper and numbered each one in no particular pattern, getting to 36. Trevor arranged his in two long lines, numbered them in order, and reported, "I grouped them by 1s and got 37."

The counts ranged from 26 to 42. Six boxes contained 39, the count that occurred most often. Before having the children figure how many raisins they had altogether in their groups, I held up a box of raisins that had not been opened or counted. I raised this question: "Suppose you were to estimate how many raisins are in this box. Based on the information I recorded on the chalkboard, what one number would be a good estimate?"

I noticed that Rick was leaning over, practically off his chair, searching

A dropped raisin gets in the way of paying attention for some children.

the floor. When I asked him what the problem was, he told me he had dropped a raisin. My immediate response to him was, "Don't worry. One raisin doesn't matter so much." This answer was clearly not satisfactory at all. Not only did Rick continue to look for the missing raisin; several of the children seated near him were beginning also to search the floor. These things happen. To avoid having the lesson totally disintegrate, I took a raisin from an extra box and gave it to Rick. Only then were he and the others ready to attend again.

I stated the question again. Their answers varied, some offering intuitive explanations for using the mode, mean, and median. Stephanie said, "I'd choose 39 because that came up most." Brandon's thought was related but different, "I'd choose 38 because even though 39 came up most, there were more guesses that were less than it, so I'd guess a little lower." Nina said, "I'd guess 37 because that seems to be in the middle." Some did not relate to the information reported. Carrie, for example, said, "I'd guess 36 because that's what I got."

Rather than pursue more formally the idea of averaging, I decided that the students would benefit from other experiences that provided the opportunity to think intuitively about averages. It is from these kinds of experiences that understanding of such concepts can be developed.

GROUP COMBINING AND SHARING

I then described their next two tasks. "You'll need to report your thinking in writing for the next two tasks. First you are to figure out how many raisins are in your group altogether and describe how you did it. Then you are to share the raisins equally, describe how many each person gets, and explain how you did the sharing."

The groups got to work quickly. Again, solutions and explanations varied. We discussed each after it was reported.

One group with three students approached the problem concretely: *We have 112 raisans.* [They showed their work for adding 39, 37, and 36.] *We decided to give the raisans one at a time. We each have 37 + 1/3 raisans.*

Another group, also with three students, avoided the problem of the extra raisin. In that group Brandon had the 39 raisins: *We have 112 raisins altogether. We added 37, 36, 39. Each of us got 37 raisins. Brandon took two away and gave one too Rick. We gave the extra one to Mrs. Hunn.*

A group with four students wrote the following, inventing a procedure that is the standard division algorithm without the symbolism: *We have 146 raisins altogether. We added all the numbers up. Everybody gets 36 1/2 each. We devided 100 into 4 parts. We each had 25. Then we took apart the 40. Then we had 35 each. After that we took apart the six. We had 36 1/2.*

A group with three students reported: *We have 105 raisins altogether. We counted them by fives. We divided them by fives. And we all had 35 each.*

A group of four wrote: *We have 154 raisins altogether. We added it altogether. We passed it around. Sara & Carrie will give 9 to each person. Kelly will give 7 to each person. Kirsten will give 10 to each person. Each person got 35 raisins.*

They showed their work for arriving at 35 by adding 18, 7, and 10. The addition was done twice. First they arranged the numbers so that the 7 was in the tens place, producing a sum of 98. That was crossed out and rewritten, the second time producing a sum of 35. This is a wonderful example of noticing an error because of the context of the problem—it didn't make sense for each person to get 98. The eventual answer, however, was still incorrect, leaving 14 raisins somehow unaccounted for.

EXTENDING TO THE LARGER BOX

Finally I gave each group a larger box of raisins, the 1 1/2-ounce size, and asked that they try to figure out how many were in this larger box and again record their thinking. Their conclusions were varied.

For a box this big [they had made an actual-size illustation of the 1 1/2-ounce raisin box] *we agreed on 117 raisins in the box. We looked at the net wt. and it was 1 1/2 oz. And we also used the little box to measure.*

Names Nina C. Ben Nick Lucy

We have 146
raisins altogether. We
added aH the numbers up.
Everybody gets 36½
each. We devided 100 into
4 parts. We each had 25.
Then we took apart the
40. Then we had 35 each.
After that we took apart
the six. We had 36½

Brandon, Ricky and Ryan
We have 112 raisins altogether.
We added 37, 36, 34.
Each of us got 37 raisins.
Brandon took two away and
gave one too Rick.
We gave the extra one
to Mrs. Hunpi.

Kirsten, Sara, Kelly and Carrie

$$\begin{array}{r} 2 \\ 36 \\ 39 \\ 40 \\ +39 \\ \hline 154 \end{array}$$

We have 154 raisins
altogether. We added it
altogether. We passed it
around. Sara & Carrie will
give 9 to each person. Kelly
will give 7 to each person. Kirsten
will give 10 to each person.

$$\begin{array}{cc} 18 & 18 \\ 7 & \\ +10 & 10 \\ \hline 95 & 35 \end{array}$$

Each person got 35 raisins.

Kylie Tracy Trevor

We have 112 raisins.

$$\begin{array}{r} 2 \\ 39 \\ +37 \\ 36 \\ \hline 112 \end{array}$$

We decided to give the 112
raisins one at a time.
We each have 37⅓ raisins.

Groups explain how they combined their raisins and shared them equally.

From the group of three that had 112 raisins altogether: *105 raisins in the big box. We took three small boxes and put them on the big box and there were about 7 left over from the 112 out of all three.*

We guess there is about 95 raisins in the big box. We sized three little boxes up with the big box. We added all the amounts of raisins in three little boxes and it ended up to about 95 raisins in all. We guess there is about 95 raisins in the big box in all.

99 because it took two and a half little boxes to fill up the big box.

Their conclusions were rough, but their discussions were animated and exciting to observe. Their methods included using the statistics already collected, comparing the sizes of the boxes, and a combination of the two. When using the statistics, some students referred to their own previous counts, while others used the record of class counts on the chalkboard. When comparing the sizes of the boxes, some groups made use of the $\frac{1}{2}$-ounce and $1\frac{1}{2}$-ounce information on the boxes, some physically compared the boxes, and some did both.

LOOKING BACK

All in all, the raisin activities provided a variety of benefits. Listening to the students discuss and come to conclusions gave me insights into their thinking, their capabilities, and their differences. As a result, I can assess their needs and make decisions about what future experiences to provide.

For example, the group that intuitively used the long division algorithm shared 146 by dividing the 100 first, then the 40, then the 6. What would they have done if the numbers hadn't been so "nice," if they had had to share, for example, 135 raisins? I'd like to know this.

Another group shared the raisins by 5s, while a third group doled them out by 1s. What would those groups do if they faced a problem without the concrete materials, if they were asked, perhaps, to figure how much they would each get if they found a five-dollar bill that no one claimed and could share it? How would the first group handle this problem?

When using the textbook as the main teaching guide, the decision to teach division often is based on where that subject is in the book, not on the children's readiness. Would it be suitable for these children? From my experience with the raisin activities, I think it would be fine most likely for Nina, Nicholas, Brandon, Lucy, Dusty; for others, perhaps; but certainly not for Molly, Ryan, or Sara.

It is the teacher's assessment of the students' abilities that is key to making instructional decisions. It is the children who should be the regulators of the curriculum, not the textbook. This activity models how assessments of children's readiness can be made during learning situations when the children are actively involved exploring problems and using mathematics skills and concepts.

The benefits to the children from this experience were that they were solving problems, thinking, writing, and using mathematics. I cannot measure what each child learned, nor would I want to. My lesson objective was not that children master a particular skill. Rather it was to provide a learning opportunity in which children's mathematical thinking could be stretched as they deal with arithmetic operations, statistical ideas, proportional reasoning, and comparison of measurements of volume and weight, all in a problem-solving situation.

Who learned most from this experience? Perhaps Trevor, one of the students, benefited most concretely. He reported: "My Mom puts raisins in my lunch sack. She buys a big bag and fills the little boxes. She's been cheating me. I never get more than 17 raisins when she fills it up. I'm going to tell her when I get home."

LOOKING AHEAD

Though the lesson was valuable, it was too much to squeeze into one day. It seems that a better plan would be to spend two lessons and not race the students through quite so much. The following plan might be a better one:

Lesson 1.

1. Show a small box. Have the students guess how many raisins it contains; then ask them to report their predictions.
2. Distribute the boxes. Students open the boxes, count what they see, and make an estimate. They then discuss their estimates in their groups, decide upon a group estimate, and report their estimate in writing, explaining their reasoning.
3. Students count their raisins, arranging them on paper so it is easy to see how many there are. You record their counts on the chalkboard.
4. Based on the information you have recorded on the chalkboard, students predict what one number might be a good guess for how many raisins are in another box. Have them record this prediction individually, explaining their reasoning. They should then discuss their thinking in their groups and finally report to the class.
5. Students figure how many raisins there are in their group altogether and record the number, explaining how they determined it. They can eat their raisins, but have them save the little boxes for the next lesson. Also save the information you recorded about their actual counts.

Lesson 2.

1. Give each group a $1\frac{1}{2}$-ounce box of raisins. Have them estimate how many raisins there are in it and explain in writing how they did this. Groups report to the class.
2. Have groups count the raisins in the box, then share them equally, again describing how they did this.

CHAPTER

•2•

INTRODUCING

MULTIPLICATION

• GRADE 3 •

"How many chopsticks would we need if four of us were eating dinner?"

Multiplication is a standard topic in the third-grade math curriculum. The traditional focus of instruction in multiplication at this grade level is on children's memorizing their times tables and practicing multiplying by one-digit multipliers, both with and without regrouping. Although children are first introduced to multiplication by learning that it is related to addition, that it is a way to do addition when adding the same number over and over again, soon the instruction concentrates on the children's learning the facts and doing paper-and-pencil computation.

Instruction that helps children develop understanding of the concept of multiplication and the ability to apply multiplication in problem situations should include a variety of experiences. A primary focus on the multiplication facts and the procedures for calculations risks having children see the facts and skills as the essence of multiplication.

Instead, instruction should surround children with experiences that foster an emphasis on understanding rather than on facts, on relationships rather than on sequential procedures. Children need to see multiplication in contexts, relate it to problem-solving situations, make use of concrete materials, investigate patterns, and relate multiplication to other areas of mathematics.

This lesson with third graders was conducted near the end of the school year. Therefore, it was not the students' initial introduction to multiplication. At the beginning of the lesson, to assess their current understanding of multiplication, children were asked to explain what they knew about multiplication. That was followed by a multiplication problem in a context, again to assess their understanding.

The children were then asked to focus on the idea that multiplication involves thinking about counting groups of objects. Working in small groups, the children were asked to identify groupings of objects from the world around them that occurred in 2s, 3s, 4s, and so on, up to 12s. The lists they generated would be used for further experiences with multiplication. How the children worked and what they put on their lists are included in the description.

The lesson is followed by a collection of activities designed to support children's continued development of understanding multiplication.

BEGINNING THE LESSON

After greeting the children, I told them the purpose of this visit. "I'm interested in hearing from you what you know about multiplication." I then asked, "What can you tell me about multiplication?"

Several hands went up. After waiting a bit to give more of the students the opportunity to collect their thoughts, I called on Trevor. "Sometimes you have to carry," he said.

I nodded and then called on Emily. "What you do is when you have a problem like 42 times 3, you times the 2 by the 3, and then you times the 4 by the 3, and that's how you get your answer."

I called on Holly next. "You don't have to use paper and pencil all the time. You learn your times tables, and then you know those."

And from Nicholas, "You get big answers. Multiplication makes numbers get big faster."

Nina, the most mathematically talented student in the class, offered, "Multiplication is when you are counting groups of things, and it helps you find out how many things you have altogether."

David gave an example, "Suppose you were buying something, like potato chips, and they cost so much each, and you were buying three of them, then you could use multiplication to tell you how much it all costs."

Stephanie focused on multiplication facts, "Some of the times tables are easy to remember, like the 5s because they all end in a 5 or 0, and some are hard to remember, like the 7s, because they're not regular."

I continued, giving all the children who wanted to contribute the opportunity to do so. The students' understanding of multiplication ranged widely, from Nina and David's grasp of the meaning and use of multiplication to most of the children's focus on the procedural aspects of the operation. All children need the chance to gain the kind of insight Nina demonstrated in her definition of multiplication and be able to identify these kinds of problem situations for which multiplication is appropriate, such as the one David illustrated.

INTRODUCING A SITUATION FOR MULTIPLICATION

I was interested in introducing an activity in which the students would focus on multiplication in contexts. Because the children seemed comfortable with the times tables, I asked the class some questions that dealt with multiples of two in order to prepare for a larger investigation of contextual situations that call for multiplication.

"If I were eating a Chinese or Japanese meal and using chopsticks," I asked the children, "how many chopsticks would I need?" They all knew that I would need two chopsticks.

I continued. "Suppose I invited three friends to dinner, and all four of us were going to eat with chopsticks. How many chopsticks would we need?" More than half the class raised their hands. Before accepting any responses, I added a direction, "When I call on you, along with giving your answer, I'd like you to explain how you figured it out."

I called on Brandon first. "It's 8, because you go 2, 4, 6, 8 for the four people," he explained, using his fingers to show the four people.

I wrote 2, 4, 6, 8 on the board and asked the class if this made sense. "Can someone else explain why what I wrote on the board tells how many chopsticks I'd need for four people?"

I called on Molly. "He just counted by 2s for the chopsticks and did that four times for the people," she explained. Other children nodded their agreement.

"Does anyone have a different way to figure the answer?" I asked.

Stephanie offered, "You do 4 times 2, and that's 8."

I wrote $4 \times 2 = 8$ on the board. "What do the 4 and the 2 have to do with my dinner party?" I asked.

Stephanie explained, "Because you have four people, and they each need two chopsticks, and that's 4 times 2."

Nicholas had another way. "You could add up the chopsticks, 2 plus 2 plus 2 plus 2, and that would give you the same answer."

I wrote $2 + 2 + 2 + 2 = 8$ on the board. "What do the 2s stand for?" I asked.

I received a chorus of answers, "The chopsticks."

"And why did Nicholas add four 2s?" I continued.

I called on Kirsten to answer. "Because there are four people."

It is important to relate numerical symbols to situations as often as possible. In this way children can come to understand that the numbers they use fit into contexts and can be explained in relation to something they can describe.

"Here's another question," I continued. "Suppose I plan to come to your class and bring a Chinese or Japanese meal for everyone. Then I'd have to figure out how many chopsticks to bring. How many students are there in the class altogether?"

"Twenty-six," Rick said.

"You'd have to bring some for Mrs. Uyeda and for you too," Nina commented.

I agreed and asked, "So how many of us will be eating in all?"

Several of the students murmured twenty-eight. I asked the class, "How can I figure out how many chopsticks to bring?"

"You have to multiply," Trevor said, making it sound as if it was an exhausting thing to have to do.

"Multiply what?" I asked.

Several children responded, "28 times 2."

"You need paper and pencil to do it," Trevor continued.

I nodded in agreement and switched the focus to an activity in which they would search for other real-world contexts for multiplication. I would return later to the computation needed to find answers.

EXPLORING CONTEXTS FOR MULTIPLICATION

"Multiplication is a way to find out how many you have altogether when things come in groups, such as chopsticks," I told the children in preparation for this activity. "What I want us to do now is to brainstorm together as a class what other sorts of things come in 2s, as chopsticks do, so we can explore other situations that call for multiplication.

"I'm going to record what you think of on a chart," I continued, and wrote on the top of a large piece of newsprint: These things come in 2s.

The children volunteered many suggestions. "Eyes." "Ears." "Hands." "Feet." "Legs." "Eyebrows." "Lips." "Nostrils." "Thumbs."

Finally I interjected, "Can you think of things that come in 2s that aren't on our bodies?"

More suggestions were offered. "Bicycle wheels." "Pedals on bicycles." "Bicycle handlebars." "Shoes." "Socks." "Gloves." "Twins." "Garbage Pail Kids." "Opposites."

The children raised questions about some suggestions. When "hands on a clock" was offered, Holly said that some watches don't have hands, showing the digital watch that she was wearing. Ben added that some clocks have three hands, like the clock in the classroom, which had a second hand.

"Hands on a clock come in 2s only sometimes," I said. "This is an important idea to pay attention to as we make our list. What I want to include on our list are things that always come in 2s, not those that only sometimes come in 2s. So I'm not going to include hands on a clock on our list."

The same sort of discussion arose when someone suggested "earrings," since they aren't always worn in pairs.

When Brandon offered "dice," I asked him to explain. "Because when you play games, you use two dice," he said.

"What about when we play the fraction game?" I asked. "How many dice do you use then?"

Several of the children responded that we use only one then, so I didn't add dice to the list.

The children continued to offer other examples. "Lenses in glasses." "Slices of bread in a sandwich." "Contact lenses." "Pairs of anything." "Wings on a bird."

"Could I write 'tricycle wheels' on our list?" I asked.

I received a chorus of no's.

"On what list would it belong?" I asked, an easy question for them. I gave a few other examples of things that would belong on different lists. "Where would I have to write 'legs on spiders'? What about 'eggs in a dozen'?"

Then I presented an exploration for them to do in small cooperative groups. I explained what I wanted to do. "I want you to think about things that come in groups other than 2s," I said, "such as the examples I just gave about tricycle wheels and legs on spiders and eggs in a dozen. I want you to think about things that come in 3s, 4s, 5s, 6s, 7s, 8s, 9s, 10s, 11s, and 12s." I wrote the numbers on the board as I said them. We counted to determine that there were ten different lists that they would need to investigate.

I continued with the directions. "You'll work together in groups. I'm going to give each group one piece of large newsprint." I had sheets of twelve-inch-by-eighteen-inch newsprint ready. "I want you to work together in your groups to organize all ten lists on this one sheet of paper and think of as many things that would fit on as many of the lists as you can. After I've given you some time to do this, I'll interrupt you, and we'll compare what different groups have come up with."

After answering the questions a few students had, I gave each group a sheet of paper, and the students got busy. I circulated and observed.

GETTING STARTED

It was fascinating to watch the groups grapple with the problem of how to organize their papers for the ten lists. I was curious about how they would handle this task and realized quickly that it was a complicated spatial problem for all the groups. Though giving the students a dittoed form or telling them how to set up their paper might have saved ten minutes or so,

3's	4's	5's	6's	7's	8's	9's	10's	11's	12's
Trickle wheek lights on a stop-light cannel tennis balls triangle sides Ian has three letters	Sqare rectangle sides wheels on trops cars truck bikes whith traning wheels Seas has frow letters legs on a dog	fingers toes	eyes ona spider Trever has six leqters incets have 6 legs	seven red lins on flag	Sp leg s plc eye		decads have ten years		oz eggs

Working together to learn about multiplication, students identify groupings of real-world objects.

the children would have been robbed of the opportunity to solve this problem. And I would have missed the chance to watch them as they struggled to organize their papers.

It was a delight to watch. It was a reminder not only of the problem-solving benefit of having students responsible for organizing their own work, but also of the creativity and uniqueness of children's thinking. The groups solved the problem in a variety of ways.

Several groups folded the paper in half, folded it again, and folded it again, each time opening it to count how many spaces there were. After three folds, there were eight spaces, in a four by two array. This was perplexing to them, and they dealt with it in several different ways.

In one group Stephanie came up with the solution of putting eight of their lists on one side, then turning the paper over for the last two lists.

In another group David folded the paper once again and opened it. The rest of the group seemed annoyed with David when they counted and found they had sixteen sections. David, however, came up with a solution that satisfied them: he labeled ten of the sections for their lists and ignored the other six.

Another group, determined to find a way to get ten sections, continued folding the paper this way and that until the paper was a mass of folds and the group was discouraged and frustrated. Finally Nicholas drew lines, eyeballing it, and divided the paper into a five-by-two array of sections somewhat the same size.

One of the other groups folded the paper in half, half again, and half once more, with all folds in the same direction. They got to the stage where they had eight columns and were stumped. Dusty solved the problem for this group by folding the first two columns in half, saying he would write small enough for these narrower spaces.

Another group had the problem solved fairly quickly because Rick seemed to be the only one interested in organizing the paper. He drew lines to get ten columns, stopping several times along the way to count how many columns he had, looking ahead across the sheet to get the columns as even as possible.

The last group was hesitant to fold or mark the paper until they had a plan. They got some smaller sheets of newsprint, and each child experimented by folding the smaller sheets. They came up with all sorts of solutions, dividing sheets of paper into six, eight, nine, twelve, and sixteen sections. They were totally stymied, and I finally intervened. "How about if I help you organize your sheet so you can get started making your lists?" I offered. They agreed with grateful sighs. I penciled their large sheet into ten sections and focused them on finding entries for the ten lists.

Interestingly, it was not apparent to the students that ten sections could be made in two rows of five each. It would seem to me that children who had been studying multiplication would see that as obvious. This reminded me that it's important to be careful when making assumptions about what children understand. It also reaffirmed how valuable problem-solving situations are for assessing students' understanding, even when incidental to the goal at hand. Also, I could see that it would benefit children to experience activities in which they would relate multiplication to rectangular arrays, so they had a way to see multiplication in a geometric context.

Once the groups had each organized their papers, they eagerly concentrated on finding entries for their lists. As with organizing their papers, groups worked differently on this part of the task. The children in some groups worked together, first thinking about things to write on the 3s list, then the 4s, and so on. Other groups worked together, but thought about things that could be written on any list, their ideas sparking each other to think of other ideas. The members of one group worked independently, each writing items on the appropriate list, with little group discussion.

One group began wandering about the room, looking for possible things. Molly excitedly reported a find, "Rulers! There are twelve inches on each ruler. There's something for the 12s list."

"Sh!" Kirsten, one of Molly's group members, said. "They'll hear you and put it on their lists." Kirsten is often competitive in class, so her response did not surprise me.

Groups also differed in how they handled the recording. In some groups there was one recorder. In others different children took turns.

Finally, I interrupted them so we could investigate what we had found.

SUMMARIZING THE ACTIVITY

I explained the procedure I wanted to use to report their entries. I wanted them to listen to each other and to think about others' ideas.

"Here's what I want us to do now," I began. "We'll go around the room, group by group. Each group will report just one thing from any one list, without telling which list it's on. Then the others in the class will have the chance to decide where it belongs. Once we agree, I'll write it on the board under the correct number.

"Also," I continued, "I want you to report something that hasn't already been suggested, so take a moment now to choose several items you'd like to report, so that you'll have an alternative if the one you chose has already been mentioned."

My goal here, as well as investigating things in the world that occur in groups as a basis for exploring multiplication, is to continue to involve the class in a thinking activity. By summarizing in this way, the children are encouraged to listen to each other, and they have the opportunity to classify each suggestion.

The groups tried to report those things they thought were unique. They seemed disappointed when they reported something and someone from another group announced, "We've got that on our list too." The offerings reported included quintuplets, players on a baseball team, wings on a butterfly, cards in a pack of Garbage Pail Kids, cans in a six-pack of Coke, red stripes on the U.S. flag, pennies in a nickel, letters in the word *car*, balls in a can of tennis balls, legs on an octopus.

Some offerings caused disagreement. The first to do so was "sides on a stop sign." The class was divided as to whether there were six sides or eight. I wrote "stop sign" off to the side as an item to be questioned later. This list of questionable items grew. "Members on a soccer team" was included because the children said when they played in school, the size of teams varied because sometimes children were absent. "Eyes on a spider" was another dispute. These would have to be verified later with research.

Some of the offerings did not fit any list because they were similar to Brandon's suggestion that dice be included on the 2s list. For example, "legs on a stool" was offered by one group, but children said a stool could have three legs or four. "Sails on a sailboat" was suggested, but some of the children knew that not all sailboats have the same number of sails.

Other offerings had to be clarified. "Points on a star" was offered by one group. Nicholas commented that not all stars had the same number of points. So the group changed its suggestion to "points on the stars on the American flag." "Numbers in a telephone number" had to be further clarified as to local or faraway numbers.

Some offerings were surprise stumpers, even to me. "Holes in a shirt," Emily offered for her group. Some of the children figured out that it belonged on the 4s list. I was still perplexed. Emily explained, pointing out four openings — at the neck, at the bottom, and at each sleeve.

How many eyes?
8 × 2 = ?

Counting eyes is one way to use the children to generate multiplication problems.

It was time for recess, and I asked the children to post the group lists so that everyone could have the opportunity to read the rest of the ideas later. I told them that the lists would be used for further activities and that it would be useful for them to be familiar with the ideas that others had had.

GENERATING MULTIPLICATION PROBLEMS

The lists are a rich resource for generating problems that the children can solve. One way to begin is to choose something from a list that can be counted on the children – eyes, for example. Pose a problem: How many eyes are there on eight children? The purpose here is not only to arrive at an answer, but also to link the problem to multiplication and to connect it to the standard symbolization. Though this problem would be simple for these third graders, who have studied the times tables, it is still valuable to reinforce the connection between the problem and what they have learned.

Ask eight children to come to the front of the room, and together count their eyes. Count by 1s. Count by 2s. Write the appropriate multiplication sentence on the board: $8 \times 2 = 16$. Relate this sentence back to the

Once there was a turtle with 20 children. She wanted to buy them some shoes but she didn't know how many shoes to buy. Help Mrs. Turtle.

Students write and illustrate multiplication problems for others to solve.

situation — eight children have two eyes each, with eight children there are sixteen eyes altogether.

Pose other problems using the children and handle them in the same way: How many ears on seven children? How many fingers do six children have? How many noses in the room altogether?

Introduce problems that do not use the children, but do use other entries from their lists. Give the children counters to use to figure them out. And be sure to link every problem to its proper multiplication sentence, each time having the children relate the numbers in the sentence back to the situation. For example, ask: How many Cokes in three six-packs? Children can use counters to show the Cokes in the six-packs.

If the students are able, have them tell you what sentence to write. If not, you write $3 \times 6 = 18$ on the board. Ask: What does the 6 tell us? What does the 3 tell us? What does the 18 tell us? How do you know that 18 is correct? Other examples: How many wheels on six tricycles? (Notice that the sentence for the tricycles is $6 \times 3 = 18$, rather than the way the same numbers are written for the cans of Coke.) How many legs on five cats? How many eggs in two dozen? How many years in four decades?

Some problems can also be solved with drawings: How many points on five stars? How many tennis balls in three cans? How many legs on four spiders?

When you have done a number of these problems and you feel the students have sufficient understanding, ask them to make up problems. You can ask them to write the problem and illustrate it on one side of the paper, then turn it over and write the complete multiplication sentence on the other side. That way the children can read each other's problems, solve them, and then check their solutions. The teacher must make sure the problems the children do are correct, but after that, if students get a problem wrong, direct them to go to the person who wrote the problem for an explanation.

It is important to note that the solution is more than the answer that results from the multiplication; it is the entire multiplication sentence. The emphasis here is on relating the multiplication sentence to the problem situations to develop children's understanding. Too often the goal is learning multiplication facts and procedures before the concept is fully understood.

INVESTIGATING PATTERNS IN MULTIPLES

The lists the children have made can also be used to generate a study of patterns in multiples and a way to introduce the students to the idea of functions. For example, use the children to investigate patterns as they count ears. Have one child come up and record $1 \times 2 = 2$ as the sentence that describes that one child has two ears, and that is two ears altogether. Have another child come up; then ask for a sentence that tells how many ears these children have altogether. Relate $2 \times 2 = 4$ to the situation that two children each have two ears, and that makes four ears altogether.

Continue for another child, and then another, until you have written sentences to account for at least a dozen of the children:

$$1 \times 2 = 2 \qquad 2 \times 2 = 4 \qquad 3 \times 2 = 6$$
$$4 \times 2 = 8 \qquad 5 \times 2 = 10 \qquad 6 \times 2 = 12 \qquad \text{and so on.}$$

Investigate the pattern of the numbers in the ones place as the multiples increase. Investigate the pattern of the numbers in the tens place. Ask the children what other patterns they notice. Have them color in these multiples on a 0–99 or 1–100 chart and describe the visual patterns.

Do a similar investigation for other multiples, each time choosing something from their lists as a way of relating the investigation to some context from the real world.

When you think the children are ready, have them work in groups to investigate the patterns in another situation. Post the directions for them to follow:

1. Choose something from a list to investigate.
2. Write a list of at least twelve multiplication sentences, for 1 times, 2 times, 3 times, etc.
3. Look for patterns in the multiples. Write about the patterns you find.
4. Color in the multiples on a 0–99 chart. Continue the pattern to the end of the chart.

WRITING MULTIPLICATION STORIES

Children benefit from continued experiences in relating situations to multiplication. Besides exploring multiplication from the lists, students can write stories that fit multiplication sentences. Each story should end with a question that can be answered by the multiplication sentence.

As with all tasks, it is important that the teacher model for the children what it is they will be expected to do. To introduce this experience, write a multiplication sentence on the board; $7 \times 3 = 21$, for example. Tell a story that ends with a question that can be answered by this sentence. Following is a sample.

> Billy was sent home from school because he was sick. His dad took him to the doctor, who told him he would have to go to bed and rest until he was well. The doctor prescribed some pills for Billy to take to help him get well. He told Billy he would have to take three pills a day for one week. How many pills would Billy have to take?

Then have each child write a different story for that same multiplication sentence. When they are finished, they should read their stories aloud to each other in their small groups. After each student reads a story, the others in the group verify whether the story ended with a question and if the question could be answered by the multiplication sentence. After the groups have finished, allow time for students who wish to do so to read their stories to the entire class.

To follow up this activity, have students write stories for other multiplication sentences, either ones they choose themselves or ones they draw from an envelope. Again, model a story for the students.

> Sara was making party favors for the six guests who would be attending her birthday party. She was wrapping small surprises in tissue paper and tying the packages with pieces of ribbon. She figured she needed eight inches of ribbon for each favor. How many inches of ribbon does Sara need to buy?

These stories can be used in several ways. Students can read their stories aloud in their small groups so others can try to give the sentence that matches. The stories can be used as activity cards or at a learning center for others to try. Also, the stories can be displayed on a bulletin board for students to read.

ANOTHER INVESTIGATION OF MULTIPLICATION IN CONTEXTS

When I was talking with the class about chopsticks and presented the problem of how many chopsticks I'd need for all twenty-eight of us, I wasn't as interested in the answer as I was in developing the idea that multiplication is useful for counting things that come in groups. However, developing ways to find the answer is important, and it is valuable to return to the chopstick question.

Before resorting to paper-and-pencil computation, however, I think it is important to deal with multiplication mentally. Thus, a reason for the traditional algorithm can be introduced.

I tried this with the children. "Remember when we were talking about chopsticks a while ago?" I asked. I continued after they nodded. "We never did figure out that day how many chopsticks I would need if all twenty-six of you plus Mrs. Uyeda and I were going to eat together. I want to think about this problem together, but without using paper and pencil. I'd like you to think along with me before we do any writing."

After getting their attention, I asked them for how many people I needed chopsticks, and several answered 28.

"Hmmm," I said, "that's a bit tricky. If there were only 10 of us, that would be easy for me. Who knows how many chopsticks I'd need for 10 people?"

Most of their hands went up, and I asked them all to say the answer together.

"What if I got chopsticks for another 10 people?" I continued. "I'd need another 20 chopsticks. So how many altogether for the two 10s?" This time I had individual students respond and explain their answers.

Nicholas said, "You'd need 40, because 20 and 20 more makes 40."

Nina answered, a bit impatiently, "You can multiply that in your head, 20 times 2 gives you 40."

"OK," I said, "if I have 40 chopsticks, then I have enough for 20 people. But there are 28 of us altogether. How many more people do I need chopsticks for?"

Some of the children volunteered that there were 8 more people. Because I felt that some of the slower children had just gotten lost, I asked the class to help me do some recording on the board. I wrote:

For 10 people, I need 20 chopsticks.
For 10 more, I need 20 more chopsticks.
So for 20 people, I need 40 chopsticks.

But there are 28 people altogether.
So I still need chopsticks for 8 more people.

This recording helped with some, but I suspected a few were still lost. However, this was the first example, and I decided to continue, knowing that there would be other opportunities for the children to think about similar problems when I got them working in their small groups.

"How many chopsticks will I need for the last 8 people?" I asked. Because they had been studying their times tables, they knew that 16 chopsticks were needed.

Some of the children excitedly called out the answer, having figured that 40 plus 16 is 56. I continued, however, recording on the board as I spoke. "See if this makes sense. I need 16 more chopsticks for the last 8 people, and I needed 40 chopsticks for the other 20 people, so altogether I'll need 56 chopsticks."

Reasoning in this way involves the application of the distributive property, a help when doing multiplication calculations mentally. However, I knew that this one example did not provide sufficient experience for the students to grasp the concept.

Next I wanted to figure out how many legs on 36 dogs. I led into the problem gradually, beginning by asking them if they knew how many legs there were altogether on 10 dogs. This was easy for them.

"What about for 100 dogs?" I asked. "Is this too hard to do?" It wasn't hard for them, and they answered with a chorus of 400.

"There are 400 what?" I said.

I called on Holly. "There are 400 legs on 100 dogs," she said.

"What about for 20 dogs?" I asked next.

Rick answered, "That would be 80 legs, 40 for 10 dogs and 40 for 10 more dogs."

"What about for 36 dogs?" I continued.

We worked this out as we had done for the chopsticks, figuring that there were 120 for 30 dogs and 24 more legs for 6 dogs.

I planned to do other such examples on future days, then give them similar problems to solve in their small groups, just by discussing, without using pencil and paper. I present these to the children as "hands on the table" solutions rather than "using paper and pencil" solutions.

Following are some other examples:

If I promised to give each student in the class five markers, how many markers would I have to buy?

If a company manufactures twenty-five tricycles a day, how many wheels a day are needed?

If you will each get three tickets for our class play, how many tickets will our class use altogether?

If a company has to paint the word *Stop* on sixteen signs, how many letters will be painted?

It is beneficial to establish proficiency with these types of problems before the standard algorithm is presented. They provide experience with multiplying by the ones and the tens and combining them, which is what the standard algorithm requires.

Also, for older children the same sort of problems can be presented, but with larger numbers. For example, if a company has twelve buses that seat forty-two people each, how many passengers can be traveling at one time? In this way you build some beginning understanding of the partial products of the standard multiplication algorithm with two-digit multipliers.

Children solve the problem of sharing six cookies among the four of them.

Children have had many experiences with fractions before they receive formal instruction in school. They drink half their milk, they share a snack with two friends, they fold paper into four parts, they learn that four quarters make a whole dollar. From these types of experiences, in which they use fractional parts and the language of fractions, children begin to develop understanding of fractional concepts.

Their understanding, however, may be limited. It is not uncommon for children to say, for example, "Your half is bigger than mine" and not notice any mathematical inconsistency. Also, their experience most likely has not helped them learn about the symbolization of fractions or about the idea of equivalence of fractions.

This lesson with third graders presents an introductory classroom experience with fractions. It was conducted in December and was the first instruction in fractions the children had during the school year. The lesson models how a problem-solving approach using concrete materials can develop children's understanding of a new concept.

In small groups children are presented with the problem of sharing cookies equally. Using paper circles to represent the cookies, the children are given the opportunity to deal with fractional concepts concretely. After their concrete exploration, the children's experience is connected to the standard symbols for writing fractions. The notion of equivalence is also introduced as an extension of the students' concrete investigation.

PRESENTING THE ACTIVITY

Before I started the lesson, I organized the class into six groups, five groups with four in each and one group of five. After settling the children, I gave them a general idea of what they would be doing.

"I'm going to give you a math activity to explore in your groups that will involve sharing cookies," I explained. Their eyes lighted up. I then gave them the bad news. "We won't be using real cookies. We'll be using make-believe cookies." They looked a bit disappointed, but they were still curious about what I would have them do.

"I've cut many small paper circles for cookies that you'll be using for this activity," I explained, showing them the circles. The circles were cut from buff-colored ditto paper and were about two inches in diameter. "You'll also have worksheets on which your groups will record your work.

"Before passing out any materials," I continued, "let me ask you a question. If I gave a group of four children four cookies to share equally, how much would each person get?" As I had predicted, this was obvious to them. But it gave me the chance to discuss sharing equally, an important concept for dealing with fractions.

I then told them that they would have a similar problem to solve in their groups. "Your first task will be to figure out how to share six cookies equally among four people. You are to use the circles I've cut as the cookies and actually share them. Use scissors; then paste each person's share on the worksheet." The worksheet had space for the group members' names at the top and was divided into four spaces in which they could paste their "cookie" shares. A question was written beneath the four spaces at the bottom of the sheet: How much did each person get?

"When you have shared the cookies," I explained further, "you are to discuss together how to record at the bottom of the sheet how much each person got."

I also told them that when they had solved the problem with six cookies, they should come and get another worksheet and try to solve the problem with five cookies, then three cookies, then two cookies, and finally with one cookie.

The goal of this lesson was to provide the children with a problem-solving experience in which they had to interact with fractional concepts. The cookies gave them the opportunity to learn from physical materials. Rather than focusing on the abstract symbolization of fractions, they could verify their thinking in the actual material they were using. Asking them to record how much each person got would give me the opportunity to learn what, if anything, the children knew about how to write fractions. I was curious how they would answer that question on their worksheets.

I asked that one member of each group come up for the group's materials, and I gave each of them six circles and a worksheet.

DURING THE WORK TIME

When they began their explorations, all groups were able to work with ease. I worried a bit that perhaps this activity was too easy for them, but the children were involved and interested. Not only did they focus on the mathematics in the activity, some groups also decorated their cookies; so some had chocolate chips, and others made raisin cookies.

They worked without interruption for about half an hour. In that time each group of four did all the problems, with six, five, three, two, and one cookies, and several groups asked for more to do. As an additional problem for those groups who finished first, I asked them to share seven cookies among four people.

When I presented the seven-cookie problem to one group, Stephanie commented that it was too easy to do. "Let us do eight cookies," she said. And then she continued thinking aloud, "But that's even easier; it would be two cookies." And then the group started to think aloud together. "What about nine cookies?" "Easy, two and a quarter." "Ten would be two and a half." Since they seemed involved and self-directed, I left them, and they didn't even notice.

I gave one particularly interested and speedy group the problem of sharing seven cookies again, but this time I said that I too, was going to attend their party, so they needed to divide it equally among five people. They did not think the problem was difficult. Though they were satisfied with their solution, it revealed that they were unable to deal with these particular fractional parts. They had pasted my share on the back of the paper and had recorded: *Evrywon get 2 halfs 1 quarter and one sliver.*

The group with five students had difficulty that I was not immediately aware of. They began by assuming that each person in their group needed a share, a decision that is commendable for its sense of fairness. It meant, however, that they had to tackle the problem of sharing six cookies among five people as their first problem. It was difficult for them, and once I noticed their struggle, I suggested they include me as well and share four cookies among the six of us. They did fine with that, but it was the only problem they had time for during the half hour. Because of their different experience, the summarizing was not very valuable for them.

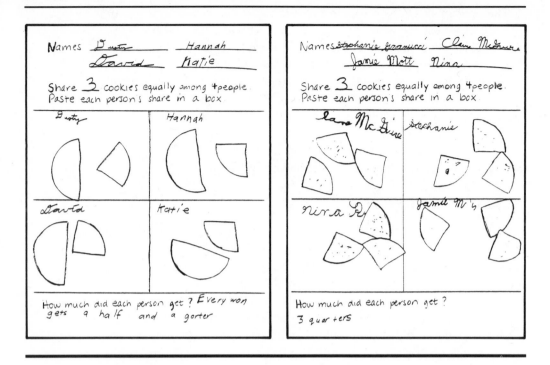

Groups find different ways to solve the problem of sharing three cookies among four children.

DISCUSSING THEIR WORK

The lesson was a rich one for summarizing. First I discussed with the children how they had organized themselves for working. The children reported the different ways they divided up the jobs of cutting, pasting, and writing; how they took turns; how they helped each other. The children had worked cooperatively in a totally natural way because their teacher had taken the time to develop the classroom atmosphere that supports such behavior, working hard to develop the children's attention to the social skills needed for cooperation.

Then I began a discussion of the fractions with the six-cookie problem. They had all reached the same conclusion—each person gets 1½. Most groups wrote the answer in words; two groups had used symbols. "So," I concluded, "you all agree on each person's share. Here's how we write it." I wrote 1½ on the board, and all the children nodded that they were familiar with those symbols. In this way I connected the standard symbolism, with which they were familiar, to their thinking in this situation.

With the five-cookie situation, a child from each group read what they had recorded to indicate each person's share. "A whole cookie and a quarter of a cookie." "One and a quarter." "Everyone gets one and a quarter." None of the groups used symbols in the recording, however.

"One of four equal pieces is one-fourth of a cookie."

I took this opportunity to introduce the symbolism. "Does anyone know how to write the fraction for one-quarter?" I asked.

Brad volunteered hesitantly, "Three over one?" This response did not surprise me. Children do not always think that the symbolism is supposed to make sense and often resort to guessing.

I decided this was a good time to explain fractional symbols to them. "Let me explain to you why one-half is written as a 1 over a 2," I said, writing ½ on the board. I took a circle and cut it into two equal pieces. "The 2," I said, pointing to the denominator, "tells us that we cut the cookie into two pieces. The 1 on top tells how many pieces I have. If I have half a cookie, I have just one of the two pieces." I did not introduce the words *numerator* and *denominator*. Instead, I referred to the cookies as the reference for the children and drew a diagram of what I had just done on the board next to where I had written ½.

I continued with fourths. "Here's how you divided a cookie into four equal parts," I said, cutting a circle into quarters. "To write how much one piece is, I need to write a 4 on the bottom. Who can explain why?" Several children volunteered. "And what do I write on top?" I continued. In this way I showed them the symbolism for one-fourth. I used the language of

Names **Claire McGuro** **Jamie M**
Nina R **Stephinie**

Share **2** cookies equally among 4 people.
Paste each person's share in a box.

How much did each person get?
Each person gets 4 halves of a quarter
of a cookie.

Though most groups share two cookies by giving each child half of a cookie, this group cuts each of their halves into smaller pieces.

one-fourth and one-quarter interchangeably as I talked. Again, I was connecting their experience to the standard fractional notation.

When I asked the groups to report how they had shared three cookies among four people, most agreed that each person got a half and a quarter, and I wrote those on the board as $1/2 + 1/4$. One group, however, reported that each person got three quarters. They had cut each of the three cookies into four quarters. Each student had taken one of the quarters from each cookie, so each had three quarters. This explanation gave me the opportunity to introduce the symbolism for three-quarters and to introduce the idea of fractional equivalence.

"Though the answers are different," I asked them, "did each group divide up the cookies equally?" There was some initial disagreement and confusion. Dusty finally blurted out, "They're just the same amount of cookie, except some people get more pieces." I took a half and a quarter of a cookie and showed how I could cut the half and wind up with three pieces, each one a quarter. I also drew a diagram of this on the board as another way to show that $1/2 + 1/4$ is the same amount as $3/4$.

As I continued to discuss each problem, I wrote the fractions on the board to connect the children's findings to the symbolism. The most interesting variation came from Claire, Jamie, Nina R., and Stephanie's solution to sharing two cookies among the four of them. Most groups had solved this problem by giving each person half a cookie. But this group cut each of their halves into smaller pieces. First they cut each half in half and knew they had two quarters. Then they cut each quarter in half. Their final conclusion stated: *Each person gets 4 halves of a quarter of a cookie.* Complicated, for sure, but understood clearly by the group.

I was pleased with the quality of the children's thinking during this lesson. Not only did the children seem to learn, but also I gained insights into their understanding.

After playing the game one time, few children put counters on 2, 11, or 12.

Probability is a topic that does not receive much, if any, attention in the standard elementary math curriculum. Several reasons explain this. Helping children master computation skills absorbs a great deal of the instructional time available. Textbooks pay little attention to probability and therefore do not offer instructional help with the topic. Also, teachers may not have a strong understanding of probability and therefore do not feel comfortable incorporating it into their instruction.

Ignoring probability is missing an opportunity to enrich children's mathematics learning. Not only are concepts in probability basic to a well-rounded education in mathematics, experience with probability contributes to developing students' critical thinking skills. Probability activities push children to devise ways to deal with uncertainty and provide opportunities for them to formulate and test ideas. In addition, experiments in probability provide contexts in which students apply the arithmetic they are learning.

Children's initial experiences with probability need to come from problem situations. An abstract approach to probability theories is not appropriate for children in the elementary grades. Instead, children should first be involved with experiments in which their intuition is developed. Once they sense what "should happen" in a situation, then children can be challenged to test the validity of their ideas.

This lesson uses dice to model an experience with probability that is appropriate for children in the elementary grades. Most children are familiar with dice, having used them to play games at home, generally for moving counters on board games. Through playing these sorts of games, children may have developed some intuitive ideas about which sums come up more often than others. This lesson builds on the children's informal experience with dice. Students are taught to play a game with two dice and then are asked to devise a winning strategy for it. The activities in the lesson focus the children on investigating the probabilities of the sums that come up when two dice are tossed.

The goal in this lesson is not to teach students the formal mathematics used to find probabilities for each of the sums. Rather, it provides students informal experiences with several probability concepts. The two-dice game gives students the opportunity to confront a situation where outcomes are not equally likely. A follow-up activity has the children collect data about the sums in order to investigate how often each sum occurs. The children are then asked to analyze the data, make inferences, and apply their analyses of the probability to their game strategies.

The lesson described was conducted with third graders. Following the description of the lesson are a synopsis of the results from the same lesson conducted in a fifth grade class and a surprising result from a class of third and fourth graders.

INTRODUCING THE LESSON

I began the lesson by holding up a pair of dice. "What do you know about these?" I asked. Many of the students were interested in responding. "They're dice." "They have dots on them, either 1, 2, 3, 4, 5, or 6." "They're square." "You use them to play games." "You roll them."

"If I roll two dice," I continued, "and figured the sum of the dots that come up, what is the smallest sum I could get?" This question elicited a chorus of 2s. I wrote a 2 on the chalkboard.

"What's the largest sum that could come up?" I asked. This time I received a chorus of 12s. I wrote the 12 on the chalkboard, leaving room for me to fit 3, 4, 5, and so on in between.

I then asked about 3. "What about 3? Is a sum of 3 possible? How could you get it?" It seemed obvious to them that you get a sum of 3 by adding 1 and 2. I continued with 4, 5, 6, and the rest of the numbers up to 12.

While verifying that these sums were all possible outcomes when rolling two dice, the students were being given the opportunity to think about the addition combinations for each of the numbers. The students who were confident with the combinations were the main contributors, though all seemed comfortable with the conclusion that the sums from 2 to 12 were possible.

"Let's see how many possible sums there are," I said. Together we counted the numbers from 2 to 12 that I had written on the chalkboard to see that there are eleven sums possible from rolling two dice.

TEACHING THE GAME

I then explained the game to the class. "I'm going to teach you a dice game that you'll play with a partner. I'm going to give you and your partner a number line with the numbers from 2 to 12 on it and eleven counters. You need to arrange your counters on your number line. You can do this any way you like. You may put one counter on each number. You may stack all the counters on one number. Or you can group them in any other way you like.

"Once all teams have placed their counters, I will begin to roll the dice. When I roll the dice, I'll call out the sum that came up. If you have a counter on that number, you remove it. For example, if I roll an 8 and you have a counter on 8, then you take it off. If you should happen to have two or three or more counters on 8, you would take off only one of those counters.

"The idea is to be the first team to remove all your counters. So I want you and your partner to talk about how you would like to arrange your counters to try to be the first team to take them all off."

I distributed the materials and watched the students sort out this task. There was some confusion with the directions, and I had to repeat them to some children. I looked around when the counters were in place. All but a few of the pairs had spread out the counters, putting one on each of the numbers. This was so pervasive that a few of the students who had begun to do something different had changed their minds when they saw what most of the others were doing.

From this I surmised that the students were not aware that when two dice are tossed, some sums appear more often than others. The idea that some events are more likely to occur than others is basic to perceiving the need for probability. I was curious to see if and how the game would change their perceptions. I also wanted to see if the students could develop any understanding of why particular sums are more likely than others.

PLAYING THE FIRST GAME

When the children had their counters ready, I began to roll the dice. After a few rolls, I had to stop and explain that they weren't allowed to rearrange their counters in the middle of the game, that they would have the chance to try a different arrangement for the next game. I continued to roll the dice, and after a short while most students had two or three counters left on their number lines.

I stopped rolling and asked one pair of students what numbers they were waiting for. They were waiting for 2, 11, and 12, they said. I asked another pair, and their answer was the same. A third pair also gave me the same response.

"Is everyone waiting for 2, 11, or 12?" I asked the class. They all nodded and seemed a bit surprised. "Maybe," I continued, "it wasn't such a good idea to put counters on those numbers. Or maybe it is just poor luck that they haven't come up."

"What sums did I call most often?" I asked. They called out what they recalled had come up most frequently. "Five." "Seven." "Eight." "Six." "Ten."

Rather than opening this for class discussion, I told them that we'd end the game and start again. "This time," I told them, "after you place your counters and before I start rolling the dice, I want you to record how you arranged the counters. That way we can compare and see what we can learn from a winning arrangement."

Their arrangements were varied this time. Few put counters on 2, 11, or 12. We played the game until we had a winner, then listened to the winners report on their winning arrangement.

Instead of continuing as a class, I gave an additional number line and two dice to each pair of children so they could play the game with each other. I encouraged them to discuss their arrangements to see what they could learn. This way I felt they would be getting several added benefits. They would become more familiar with the game. They would have to figure the sums themselves, giving them practice with basic addition facts. They could have more opportunity for discussing arrangements. They could work at their own pace.

Some of the students recorded their arrangements again, doing it in several different ways. Also, though no suggestion had been made to do so, several of the students kept track of the sums that came up as they played.

EXTENDING THE GAME

After the students had played for a while, I told them I wanted to take a break from the game and try a different, but related, activity. I had prepared worksheets for this activity, as shown, and modeled for them what I wanted each of them to do. I rolled the dice and recorded the sum with an X in the proper column. I did that for about half a dozen sums.

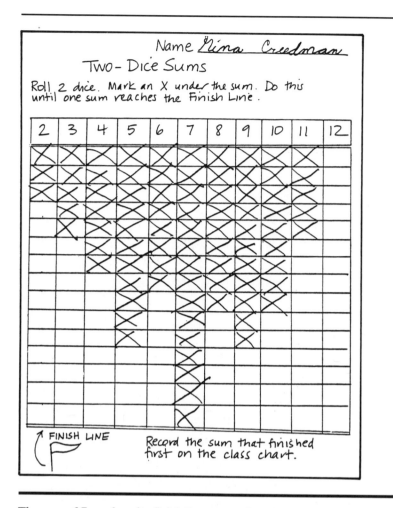

Name *Nina Creedman*

Two-Dice Sums

Roll 2 dice. Mark an X under the sum. Do this until one sum reaches the Finish Line.

2	3	4	5	6	7	8	9	10	11	12

↑ FINISH LINE

Record the sum that finished first on the class chart.

The sum of 7 reaches the finish line more often than other sums on the students' worksheets.

"When you do this," I explained, "you'll continue until one sum reaches the bottom of its column, the finish line. Then come up to the front and mark the sum that finished on the class chart." The class chart was another graph of the possible sums.

The students were eager to begin. They liked having their own dice and worksheets. Watching the children in this setting revealed differences in how they worked, and now I had the opportunity to assess how individuals approached finding the sums. Some knew the sums immediately from inspecting the two dice. Others had to count all the dots. Some started with the number on one die and found the sum by counting on the dots on the other die. Watching them work gave their teacher the chance to compare how she perceived their basic number skills with what they did when having to find sums from the dice.

Most students completed two or three sheets before I interrupted them to

The sum of 7 came up most often on the children's papers.

examine and discuss our class results. The class chart showed 7 as having finished first on an overwhelming majority of papers.

"Why do you think this is so?" I asked. Some students shrugged their shoulders. One said that 7 was his lucky number.

Nina offered a clear explanation. "The reason that 7 comes up more often is that there are more ways to get 7. There is only one way to get 12," she went on, "because you have to roll both 6s. But there are lots of ways you could get 7."

"What are the ways?" I asked.

Several others volunteered. "5 and 2." "4 and 3." "6 and 1."

"How many ways are there to get 2?" I asked.

"Only one," Trevor said. "You have to get a 1 and a 1."

"What about to get a 9?" I asked.

"Lots," Ian responded, and continued, "8 and 1, 7 and 2 . . ."

Several of the children interrupted him. Holly explained, "You can't do that. There's no 8 on the dice. There isn't a 7 either."

"How can you get a sum of 9 on the dice?" I asked again.

This time I was told 5 and 4 would work, and so would 6 and 3.

"What other sums finished first?" I asked, drawing their attention back to

```
2 3 4 5 6 7 8 9 10 11 12
```

I would put one on
each number because
On you're first turn
any number that you
would roll you could
take off one cube.

Carrie seems most interested in insuring that she will be able to remove a cube on the first roll.

Lucky: 5, 6, 7, 8,

I would put the most on
seven beaaaause their are more
ways to make seven than any
other number. But not to many.
And I dare you to put them
on 12 or 2 because they have
only one combination.

Nicholas understands that some sums have a greater probability of being rolled than others.

the class chart. Though there were many more 7s, there were a fair number of 5s, 6s, 8s, and 9s.

I could not think of a way to deal with the fact that the number of ways to arrive at any sum was more than they predicted, depending on which die came up 6, for example, and which came up with a 1. However, I decided to continue because I was interested to see how they would use the information they had gotten so far while playing the game, or even if they would use the information.

I asked the students to think about how they would now arrange the counters to try to win the game. I asked them to write descriptions of the arrangements they would use, explaining why they made those choices. There was a good deal of a variety in their thinking.

From Nicholas: *I would put the most on seven beacause their are more ways to make seven than any other number. But not to many. And I dare you to put them on 12 or 2 because they have only one combination.*

From Lucy: *I would put the most on 7. Because it has the most waes to make it. Then I would put 3 on 8 because I keep getting it. And two on 6, 3, 5, 10, and one on 11 because sometimes I get them.*

From Carrie: *I would put one on each number because on you're first turn any number that you would roll you could take off one cube.*

From Claire: *Odd numbers are easyer to roll because there are more ways to make them up.*

From Jamie: *I'd put one on eight, one on nine, one on six, one on four, two on five, one on three, one on ten, and three on seven because I won when I did it that way.*

Dusty's math understanding surpassed his writing ability: *five won a lot for me. but on the chart seven. why is becuse there is more ways to make seven than the other wons. I would poot fore on 7 and five, two on nine and one on for.*

I left the dice, the number lines, and a supply of additional worksheets with the class. The children were given time to continue playing the game. Their interest was sustained over several weeks, and they sharpened their strategies.

RESULTS FROM FIFTH GRADERS

Stephanie Sheffield presented a similar experience to her fifth graders. After she introduced the game, the students played it many times in pairs. They were then asked to explain how they would arrange the counters, based on their playing experience. They wrote their descriptions with their partners, and the thinking among pairs was quite varied.

From Joel and Katherine: *Our conclusion is that to win the game you must put the counters or beans on numbers seven eight, ten and six. Most of your counters or beans should be on numbers seven and eight.*

From Thuy and Tanya, a competitive view: *We think 7, 9, 6, and 5 are rolled the most. If your opponent puts three on one number, you would put one less than that person did. Then put the extra counters on the numbers you think are rolled the most.*

From Lawren and John, a terse but noncommittal conclusion: *John and I found out that if you put the counters on the numbers between 2 and 12, you might have a good chance of winning.*

The students were then given the worksheet to complete. A class chart of the sums that finished first on their worksheets was started. After discus-

The initial reaction from these boys pays no attention to probabilities.

sing the results from the class graph, the students were asked to describe why the class chart came out as it did.

Joel and Katherine wrote: *It turned out that way because six, seven, and eight have more addends than the rest of the numbers. Example: addends of 7 = 3, 4, 1, 6, 2, 5, addends of 2 = 1. Seven can come out more than two.*

Thuy and Tanya wrote: *The smaller numbers have less number to add up to. Examples: 2 + 1 = 3, 1 + 2 = 3. The larger #'s have less #'s, 6 + 5 = 11, 5 + 6 = 11. 7 has more #'s to add up to 7 such as 4 + 3 = 7, 6 + 1 = 7, 5 + 2 = 7.*

The students were interested in the game and continued playing it during the next two days. After that time, Stephanie gave them an individual writing assignment, asking them to explain what they had learned from playing the game.

From Tanya: *I learned it's better to put your counters on 6, 7, and 8 because those three numbers have a lot of numbers that will add up to 6, 7, and 8. Also that you shouldn't put any on 2, 12, or 11 because they don't have many numbers to add up to them.*

From Namthong: *I learned that seven came out the most on the two dice games because there are many number that make sevens. We drew this on the board.* And Namthong included a listing of all the different ways to make each of the sums.

From Jack: *I learned that for playing the counters game you should put most of the counters on 7. But I think you should put them on the numbers 5-9. You need to have other numbers for the game. You should put most of them on 7 because it has more combinations of rolled dice. But the dice won't equal 7 every time. So put some counters on the numbers 5-9 so you have a better chance of clearing your board. The numbers 5-9 are good because they have a more likely chance of being rolled than the numbers 1-4 and 10-12.*

After further exploration and class discussion, Lawren's understanding of probability grows.

From Linda: *I think that when I play this game again I think that I would put 4 on number 7 and 2 on number 6 and number 8 and 1 on number 5 and number 9 and 1 on number 4. I would put my beans on these numbers because I learned that 7 is rolled most often and 4, 5, 6, 8, and 9 are rolled often because these numbers have more numbers that = these numbers.*

Lawren wrote: *Now I have understood how 6, 7, 8, and 9 are rolled often. They are rolled often because they have more sums and numbers that add to be them. Now I will put my counters on 8, 7, 5, and 9."* Lawren drew a number line and indicated three counters on 7 and two each on 5, 6, 8, and 9.

Carman took a different approach when writing her explanation of what she had learned from the game: *In this game I've learned something. I have learned that Math is possible. I meen that I used to think that it all couldn't be done because it would take too long that it was not interesting. But in this game I have found out that it is not long and that it is interesting. And to tell you the truth, I think it was fun. And in this game I found that the 6, 7, and 8 would be the best numbers. But I think that I would still put my counters on the 3, 4, 5, 9, 10, and 11 because there is still a chance for those number to be rolled.*

Carman   Orange Grove
Math   March 21, 86

Two Dice Game

In this game I've learned something
I have learned that Math is possible.
I mean that I used to think that it all couldn't
be done because it would take too long that
it was not interesting. But in this game
I have found out that it isn't long
and that it is interesting. And to
tell you the truth, I think it was fun.
And in this game I found that the 6 and 8.
would be the best numbers. But I think
that I would still put my conters on the 3,
4, 5, 9, 10, and 11 because their is still a chance
for those number to be rolled.

Carman explains what she learned from the two-dice game lesson.

A REACTION FROM THIRD AND FOURTH GRADERS

Children in Sandra Nye's third-fourth grade class responded in a similar way to the two-dice game. They came to the conclusion that the sum of seven comes up more often when two dice are rolled and reported their strategies accordingly. And as with the other classes, the experience was one that got them involved and kept them interested.

As a follow-up activity several days later, Sandra asked the children how they would arrange counters on a number line for a game that was played with only one die. For that game only the numbers 1 through 6 were on the number line. Most of the children responded with the same strategy as for two dice — they chose to heap more of their counters in the middle, with most on the number 3 and least on the numbers 6 and 1.

After playing the game, they realized that their strategy hadn't been a sensible one. Their new understanding developed from their own experience with the game. The children's faulty strategy for the one-die game served as a reminder of how careful we need to be as teachers in making assumptions about what children understand and learn from the lessons we present. And it was a testimony that first-hand experience is the best teacher of all.

Students color in all the numbers that are multiples of 3.

The activities presented in this chapter engage children in investigating numbers arranged on a 0–99 chart. The overall goal of the activities is to build students' understanding of the orderliness of our number system and the properties of numbers. In each of the experiences, students explore the patterns that exist in this array of numbers.

Experiences such as these present a balance to the computational emphasis of most elementary math programs. They contribute to developing students' understanding of numbers by having them investigate numbers in ways that emphasize their thinking rather than their computational skills. It is beneficial for students throughout the elementary grades to have many experiences of this kind.

The activities presented are suitable and valuable for students with different abilities and in different grades. While an activity may serve to introduce a concept to some students, it can at the same time strengthen or cement the mathematical understanding of others. For that reason lessons in two different classrooms are described. One class is a third-and fourth-grade combination; the other is a sixth-grade class. Two additional suggestions for activities follow the descriptions of the lessons.

SEARCHING FOR PATTERNS WITH THIRD AND FOURTH GRADERS

The abilities of the children in this class spanned a wide range. Not only were two grade levels represented, the fourth graders had scored between the 2d and 99th percentiles in math when tested at the end of the third grade.

The children were eager learners. Their teacher gave consistent attention to their interpersonal relationships, and the children's ability to work well together in small cooperative groups reflected this attention. Students were regularly seated in small groups of four, with occasional groups of three when necessary. Groups were randomly formed and changed every two weeks.

The first activity involved children in a search for patterns on the 0–99 chart. To prepare for the activity, I reproduced a recording sheet for each student on which there were six 0–99 charts. Using a nine-inch-by-twelve-inch envelope for each group, I put recording sheets for group members in each envelope. Also in each envelope I put six strips of paper resembling large-sized fortune cookie messages, with directions on them.

I introduced the activity to the class using a 0–99 chart on the overhead projector. To model for the children how they would be expected to proceed, I reached into one of the envelopes and drew out a strip. I gave the class the direction, "Color in all the numbers whose first digits are larger than their second digits." (I did not read what was actually on the strip; I made up the direction so the children wouldn't repeat this particular one when they did the investigations on their own.)

I then asked, "Who can tell me a number on the chart that fits the direction?"

A few children raised their hands instantly, but I waited a bit, giving the others time to think. Finally I called on Melissa, who offered the number 10.

"I accept that," I responded, coloring in that number on the chart. I then asked, "Who can explain why 10 fits the direction I read?"

I had several children give explanations. Even though their explanations were similar, I felt it was valuable. Students often have difficulty explaining their reasoning and need a great deal of practice in doing so.

I continued, "Who can tell me another number that I should color in on the chart?"

This time Michael volunteered the number 32. Again I accepted the response and then had several students explain why 32 followed the direction.

The third time I asked, Brad responded with the number 4. I hesitated for a moment, not quite sure how to respond. Finally I said, "No, that doesn't fit my rule. I'd like you to discuss in your groups how you could explain to Brad why I shouldn't color in the number 4."

After their group discussions, the students offered several explanations to help Brad. It turned out that Brad had not understood what digit meant. The discussion cleared it up for him, and Brad then showed his understanding by offering a number that did fit the direction.

As a further check on students' understanding, I asked the groups to decide upon five more numbers that they thought would fit the rule and to make sure they all agreed on what the direction called for. I circulated through the class, listening for difficulties. After giving them time, I asked if there was any confusion or disagreement about the numbers. There was none.

"Let's color in some of the numbers you thought of," I said, "and see what pattern we notice." I called on groups to contribute numbers in turn, coloring them in on the chart until some of the children began to predict what was happening.

Shelley offered, "They're all on the bottom part of the chart. I think they'll all be on the bottom part."

"But what about 10?" I asked. "That doesn't seem to be on the bottom of the chart."

"Not the bottom. Under the slant," Shawn explained.

"Who can describe the pattern differently?" I probed. Several students contributed. "On the left bottom side." "From the bottom left corner to the middle." "Under the diagonal." After each contribution, I persisted, asking if anyone could describe the pattern another way, continuing to encourage the children to verbalize their thoughts.

Feeling comfortable that the children understood what we were doing, I explained the group task to the class. I told the students that there were six strips with directions in their envelopes, along with recording sheets with six 0–99 charts on each. Students were to color in their own charts. However, they were to work as a group, drawing just one direction at a time out of the envelope for everyone to do, not drawing another until all had finished that chart. I reminded them that although each student was responsible for a recording sheet, they were to discuss their work together, to look for patterns, and to try to describe the patterns they found.

The six strips of paper included the following directions:

Color in all the even numbers.
Color in all the numbers whose digits add to 8.
Color in all the numbers whose digits differ by 1.
Color in all numbers that have a 4 in them.
Color in all the multiples of 3.
Color in all the numbers with double digits.

MONITORING THE EXPLORATION

As I circulated, I noticed that the children understood the logistics of proceeding with the task. However, the directions on some strips were raising questions and causing difficulties.

One group was struggling with the direction to color in all the even numbers. Shawn noticed immediately that the even numbers were in vertical columns and told his group, "See, you just have to color down like this, in stripes." The others, however, were working differently. Brad and Kevin seemed to be picking out even numbers from the chart almost at random, comparing choices. "There's one. Here's another one." Tim was proceeding in an orderly fashion, having started with 2 and coloring in every other number, working across the rows from left to right.

Though Shawn was not successful in convincing the others right away that his method would not only work, but it would also save time, he was patient, continuing to color in the columns while observing the others. After each of the other boys had worked for a while, however, they came to the same conclusion.

Tim, however, had a question about 0. He was unwilling to include it, and when I came by, he asked me about it. I turned the question back to the group. "Is 0 an even number?" The other students didn't seem to know either.

"Does it fit the colored-in pattern of the other even numbers on your charts?" I pursued. They answered that it did fit the pattern, but didn't seem convinced by that evidence.

"How do you know if a number is even?" I continued. Kevin, a fourth grader who was one of the lowest math students in the class, responded, "It has a 2 or a 4 or a 6 or an 8 in it."

I drew the group's attention to Kevin's chart. "But you didn't color in 23, and that has a 2 in it." Kevin looked confused.

Shawn helped, "It has to end in one of those numbers. It can end in 0 too; that's why I think 0 is even."

"Another thing about even numbers," I explained, "is that they can be divided into two equal numbers. Six is even because it is the same as two 3s, 3 + 3. Eight is even because it is the same as two 4s, 4 + 4. How about 10? How about 12? Why not 5? How about 15? Now, how about 0?"

From their responses, I felt that Kevin still wasn't sure, nor did Brad seem to be. But Tim was now convinced, and he and Shawn were confident

Even numbers

0	1	2	3	4	5	6	7	8	9
10	11	12	13	14	15	16	17	18	19
20	21	22	23	24	25	26	27	28	29
30	31	32	33	34	35	36	37	38	39
40	41	42	43	44	45	46	47	48	49
50	51	52	53	54	55	56	57	58	59
60	61	62	63	64	65	66	67	68	69
70	71	72	73	74	75	76	77	78	79
80	81	82	83	84	85	86	87	88	89
90	91	92	93	94	95	96	97	98	99

Even numbers

Numbers whose digits add to 8

0	1	2	3	4	5	6	7	8	9
10	11	12	13	14	15	16	17	18	19
20	21	22	23	24	25	26	27	28	29
30	31	32	33	34	35	36	37	38	39
40	41	42	43	44	45	46	47	48	49
50	51	52	53	54	55	56	57	58	59
60	61	62	63	64	65	66	67	68	69
70	71	72	73	74	75	76	77	78	79
80	81	82	83	84	85	86	87	88	89
90	91	92	93	94	95	96	97	98	99

Numbers whose digits add to 8

Numbers whose digits differ by 1

0	1	2	3	4	5	6	7	8	9
10	11	12	13	14	15	16	17	18	19
20	21	22	23	24	25	26	27	28	29
30	31	32	33	34	35	36	37	38	39
40	41	42	43	44	45	46	47	48	49
50	51	52	53	54	55	56	57	58	59
60	61	62	63	64	65	66	67	68	69
70	71	72	73	74	75	76	77	78	79
80	81	82	83	84	85	86	87	88	89
90	91	92	93	94	95	96	97	98	99

Numbers whose digits differ by 1

Numbers with a 4 in them

0	1	2	3	4	5	6	7	8	9
10	11	12	13	14	15	16	17	18	19
20	21	22	23	24	25	26	27	28	29
30	31	32	33	34	35	36	37	38	39
40	41	42	43	44	45	46	47	48	49
50	51	52	53	54	55	56	57	58	59
60	61	62	63	64	65	66	67	68	69
70	71	72	73	74	75	76	77	78	79
80	81	82	83	84	85	86	87	88	89
90	91	92	93	94	95	96	97	98	99

Numbers with a 4 in them

Multiples of 3

0	1	2	3	4	5	6	7	8	9
10	11	12	13	14	15	16	17	18	19
20	21	22	23	24	25	26	27	28	29
30	31	32	33	34	35	36	37	38	39
40	41	42	43	44	45	46	47	48	49
50	51	52	53	54	55	56	57	58	59
60	61	62	63	64	65	66	67	68	69
70	71	72	73	74	75	76	77	78	79
80	81	82	83	84	85	86	87	88	89
90	91	92	93	94	95	96	97	98	99

Multiples of 3

Numbers with double digits

0	1	2	3	4	5	6	7	8	9
10	11	12	13	14	15	16	17	18	19
20	21	22	23	24	25	26	27	28	29
30	31	32	33	34	35	36	37	38	39
40	41	42	43	44	45	46	47	48	49
50	51	52	53	54	55	56	57	58	59
60	61	62	63	64	65	66	67	68	69
70	71	72	73	74	75	76	77	78	79
80	81	82	83	84	85	86	87	88	89
90	91	92	93	94	95	96	97	98	99

Numbers with double digits

in their understanding. This difference within the group didn't trouble me. Not only did it give me information about the boys' understanding, I know that Brad and Kevin may need many experiences before they fully grasp the concepts of even and odd. This experience can help them along. Besides, from responding to my questioning, Tim and Shawn had the opportunity to cement their already-developed understanding. When I left them, the boys reached for another of the directions.

Coloring in numbers with a 4 in them and numbers whose digits add to 8 did not trouble any of the groups. However, there was confusion in about half of the groups about what was meant by *double digits*. Some interpreted it to mean all numbers that had two digits; and they colored in all numbers larger than 9. However, other groups assumed it meant numbers with both digits the same; and they colored in 11, 22, 33, and so on down the diagonal to 99. In one group the students engaged in a disagreement, the result of which was that two of the students did it one way, and the other two did it the other way. Though both were reasonable interpretations, I had meant the students to color in numbers with both digits the same, and I made a mental note to discuss this ambiguity with the entire class later.

The word *differ* was confusing to many of the children. Though the children knew about subtraction, knew the word *difference,* and understood the idea of one more and one less, the wording in the direction did not make sense to them. I had to discuss the relationship between differ and subtraction with more than half the groups before they could proceed with finding the numbers on their charts.

Multiples of 3 also caused confusion, more so to the third graders who had had less experience with multiplication than most of the fourth graders had had. In this situation, however, the multigraded groups were a great asset. Fourth graders had the opportunity to explain to their group members; third graders had the opportunity to learn. Some children stopped their coloring of multiples of 3 at the number 30, and I helped them see how to extend the pattern.

After about half an hour, four hands went up in the group at the back of the room to tell me that they were finished. I wasn't surprised because Hai and Sara, the two strongest math students, were in that group. Each of the students in the group had finished the charts. To get a sense of their understanding, I engaged them in several ways.

First I chose at random one of the strips and said to the group, "I'll read this direction to you. See if you can show me which of your charts it matches." I did that for several of the strips. It was easy for them.

Then I asked them to describe the patterns for each chart. In doing so a good deal of geometric vocabulary emerged. "The two lines go in the same direction. They're parallel." "They're on a diagonal." "The stripes go up and down." "Yeah, they're vertical." "They're parallel too." "These two lines make a T, like a cross."

I interjected here, "Lines that make a T are called perpendicular." This

Hai is excited to tell what he discovered.

was the only comment that I added. The other comments had come from the students.

"Do you think you could make up directions for other patterns?" I asked them.

"Sure," Hai, always the first to respond, said. "We could make up lots of them."

"For now," I asked, "I'd like you to make up six additional rules. You do not each need to write them. Choose one of you to record for the group. Call me when you get all six done." I planned to give them new sheets when they were finished so they could begin to color in their own patterns. Inventing directions would give the students a valuable thinking experience that would also prepare them for a game I would teach in a later lesson.

I left the group to create their directions, but didn't get far before Hai rushed up to tell me what he had figured out. "We were going to write a rule to color in the multiples of two," he said, "but that will just give the same pattern as the even numbers." He raced back to join his group, pleased with his discovery.

It was a busy time, active and bustling for the children, demanding for me. Though there was some confusion that I had not anticipated, I saw it as an opportunity for learning, both mine and the students'. That some of the groups worked more slowly than others was not a problem. Understanding, rather than speed, was what mattered.

Because it was nearing time to go to the library, I interrupted the class. It was not easy to get the students to stop work. "If I promise you that you can get back to work on this later, can I get you to put your work away now?" I asked. "I'll give you until the count of 6 to get ready to go to the library," I said and counted slowly while the students got organized.

FURTHER ACTIVITIES

When the class returned to this activity for a second work period, I explained the extension of inventing new rules of their own once they had finished coloring in their six charts. I emphasized strongly, however, that they were to be sure to finish the original six directions before making up their own rules.

I circulated, working with the groups who were finishing the initial activity, having them describe their patterns as I had done with the group that had finished first. As groups wrote their own directions, I helped them to be clear in their descriptions and to write their directions in complete sentences. Two of the groups completed their six directions quickly, and I gave them new recording sheets so they could see what patterns their rules would generate. The other groups did not have the chance to color in their patterns during class, but all had the opportunity to invent some new rules.

In a class discussion I had the groups share the rules they had invented. Kim was particularly excited about a rule she had created. Her rule was: Color in all the numbers with a 4 in it and all the numbers with digits that add to 4. The pattern, when colored in, produced the numeral 4!

I wrote all the children's rules on a large sheet of chart paper to post in the room and put out extra sheets of 0–99 charts so those who wanted to color in patterns for different rules could do so. All this was to prepare the class for the game I planned to teach.

THE 0–99 CHART GAME

Materials were needed for the game, and I had the students help prepare them. I gave each group two pieces of tagboard. Each piece was a ten-inch square that I had ruled into a ten-by-ten array. The groups were asked to fill each with numbers just like the 0–99 chart. Not only do I believe that the students should be involved in creating materials they will be using, I think there is benefit to having them fill in these numbers.

For adults the sequence of the numbers arranged on the 0–99 chart is obvious. However, that is not so for all children. It is only after many experiences that the orderliness of the patterns emerges. When they have to fill in the numbers themselves, the order in this array of numbers can become even clearer for some of the children. It was interesting to watch the children fill in the charts in different ways, some writing the numbers in sequence, some writing them in columns, some sharing the job with a partner and starting at different places on the tagboard.

I collected the charts so I could laminate them. I then took half of them and cut them apart into the 100 numbers. The next day I gave each group an uncut 0–99 chart and an envelope that contained a set of cut-apart numbers. I explained how to play the game.

"There are three rules to follow," I began, bringing out a chart on which I had written the rules, which I would post for the students' reference. "Rule number 1 says that you are to divide up the numbers equally among the players." I elaborated, "Don't look at the numbers, just divide them up randomly. How many numbers will each person in a group of four get?" Several of the children raised their hands, and I called on one.

"What about in the group of three?" I asked. "How many will each of them get?" I told the children that if there were three of them, they should place the extra numeral on the board.

"Rule number 2," I continued. "Players take turns calling out a direction. Players place all of their numbers that fit the direction on the chart." I then explained the rule further. "On your turn, you can say any of the directions I gave you to color, or any from our posted class list of the rules you made up. Or you can invent a new direction if you like. Remember, not only does the person who says the rule play numbers on the board, but everyone in the group does.

"Rule number 3 says that you win if you are the first player to play all your numbers." I then added, "So when it's your turn, you'll want to pick rules that allow you to play as many of your numbers as possible, but won't allow another player to go out.

"Let's go over the rules again," I said, referring to the chart. "Who would like to read the first rule?" I chose Denise. I then asked who could explain what the rule meant, asking the children if they understood and if they had any questions before I repeated the procedure for the other two rules.

"Can we see each other's numbers?" Jody asked.

"Yes," I answered, "you should keep your numbers face up in front of you. And you should make sure that the numbers played by the others are correct."

"What if two people finish at the same time?" Charles asked.

"Then both count that as a win and play another game," I answered.

"How many games should we play?" Jennifer asked.

"Play as many as you have time for," I responded. "Some games will go more quickly than others."

With all questions answered, the children got busy. I circulated, having to clarify the rules for several of the groups before they all got off to a firm start. I counted on the game to help cement the children's familiarity with the 0–99 chart. Many adults can recall the design of the Monopoly board, even after years of not having played the game; they are still able to describe where, for example, the railroads or Boardwalk and Park Place or the properties with the yellow stripes are. It was from playing the game that those images were set, and it is the same result that I hope this game will accomplish.

The children were involved with the game for the rest of the class period. I made time the next day for them to play again, planning to provide time for play as long as the children stayed interested. I also made the game materials available for when the children were able to choose activities to pursue. In addition, I told the children that they could check out the game and take it home if they would like to teach their sisters and brothers and parents. If they did so, however, they would have to copy the rules and take them home as well.

ARROW ARITHMETIC WITH SIXTH GRADERS

In the 1960s David Page created activities known as Arrow Arithmetic for use with the 0–99 chart. Those activities provide another way to build familiarity with patterns on the 0–99 chart and can be effectively introduced in a whole-class lesson. Following is a description of how I used them with a class of sixth graders.

I projected the 0–99 chart for the class to see, leaving the chalkboard free, and explained to the class, "I am going to introduce something that I would like each of you to try to figure out, and I am going to do this in a special way—without any talking, either from me or from you. What I'll do to get started is to put a star, which is our signal not to speak, on the chalkboard. We'll work silently until I erase the star; then we'll discuss what happened. The reason I've planned to do this silently is so that each of you will have the chance to think without the interference of hearing others' thoughts. Eventually, we'll all share what we know. Are there any questions?"

There were no questions. I added one final comment, "What we'll be doing in this activity has to do with the numbers on the 0–99 chart. That's why I've projected it." I drew a star on the board, waited a moment for the hush to settle, then wrote on the board:

$$7 \rightarrow \; = \square$$

I tapped the chalk on the box to indicate that something ought to be written there and held out the chalk. Several students raised their hands. I gave the chalk to one of them, who came to the board and wrote an 8 in the box. I nodded my assent and wrote another on the board: $52 \rightarrow \; = \square$. Again I gave the chalk to a student, who wrote 53 in the box. I continued, varying the problems, $36 \leftarrow \; = \square$, $21 \uparrow \; = \square$, $77 \downarrow \; = \square$, until all students were raising their hands to respond.

I continued, still silently, trying variations, doing enough of each type to allow the students a chance to catch on:

$$41 \rightarrow \rightarrow \rightarrow = \square$$
$$25 \nearrow = \square$$
$$47 \searrow = \square$$
$$35 \uparrow \downarrow \uparrow \downarrow \uparrow \downarrow = \square$$
$$35 \uparrow \downarrow \uparrow \downarrow \uparrow \downarrow \rightarrow = \square$$

After about fifteen minutes, I erased the star and heard a general sigh, as if all the students in the class had been holding their breath for the duration of the activity. "Well," I asked, "what do you think?"

"That was easy." "It was fun." "The ones with the diagonal arrows were a little trickier." "It seemed so easy when I caught on, but I didn't see it at first."

Mark added, "I liked those long ones with lots of arrows. I thought they'd be hard, but those up and down arrows just cancel each other out."

I probed a bit further. "Does every arrow have another that cancels it out? What about $\rightarrow$? What about the diagonal arrows?" We identified an opposite for each arrow.

I then gave them an activity to do in their small groups. "I want each group to make up ten problems and write them on one sheet of paper. On a second sheet write the answers for your problems. Be sure to put your names on both sheets so I can keep them together. I'll collect them at the end of the period; tomorrow each group will try the problems that another group made up."

I gave one additional direction. "Vary the number of arrows in your problems, using no more than ten arrows in each one." This condition was to prevent what had occurred when I had done this activity with a class of eighth graders. Perhaps they had been a particularly zealous group, but some used so many arrows they could barely fit their ten problems on one side of a sheet of paper.

On the next day, before I distributed the groups' problems for them to solve, I explained the procedure I wanted them to follow. "I am going to give each group one of the sheets of ten problems and a 0–99 chart to refer to. When solving the ten problems, however, I'd like you to discuss each one as a group without looking at the chart and try to come to agreement on an answer. In other words I want you to try to solve the problems without tracing the paths on the chart."

Without projecting the 0–99 chart, I put a problem on the board to model what I wanted them to do: $32 \rightarrow \leftarrow \rightarrow \rightarrow \uparrow \downarrow \leftarrow = \square$. Several hands shot up immediately. "Before I call on anyone to answer," I said, "talk about this in your groups to see what you notice that can help you solve this problem without referring to a chart." In this way I was asking them to visualize the chart or to use the patterns in the arrows to come to conclusions.

When I interrupted them, I asked that they all say the answer they had found simultaneously, and I heard a chorus of 33s. When I asked them to explain how they had arrived at that answer, students pointed out how arrows cancelled each other, even when they were not next to each other, and how there was one arrow that was left over, which pointed to the right.

I passed out a sheet of problems and a 0–99 chart to each group, left the answer sheets on the counter for them to use when they had finished, and told them I would start groups on the next activity when they had completed this one.

Students enjoyed this activity, approaching the problems as puzzles to solve. As groups completed the activity, I discussed their work with them briefly. I then gave them a sheet of directions I had prepared, again for them to work on in their groups. There were three parts to this extension:

> **Part I** → can be interpreted to mean the same as + 1. Find an arithmetic interpretation for each of the other arrows. Record below.
>
> **Part II** The horizontal and vertical arrows can help when adding and subtracting numbers in your head. For example, 52 + 34 can be thought of as starting at 52 and going down three rows to add 30 and over four to the right to add 4. Try this. Do you arrive at 86?
>
> Now try 78 − 23. Go up two rows to subtract 20, which puts you at 58; then go three to the left to subtract 3. Where are you now?
>
> In your group give each other problems like this to try to solve. Note: What will you do with tricky ones that require that you change rows? For example, 37 + 25 requires that you go down two rows and over five numbers. Can you decide how to do this?
>
> **Part III** Decide as a group what might be a reasonable answer to 4↑ = □. Write an explanation describing how you arrived at your answer.

The first two parts of this sheet were designed to relate the structure of the chart to its usefulness for mental computation. The third part was a challenge for them because we had not studied positive and negative numbers. The students were accustomed to these types of questions, however, and knew that they weren't being given a test for a correct response, but a challenge to get them thinking about something new. Their thoughts would be discussed when the activity was summarized with the entire class.

These Arrow Arithmetic problems accomplish the same goal as do coloring in patterns—focusing students on the orderly array of the 0–99 chart. Third graders could just as easily do this activity without, perhaps, the extension into the mental computation. Able sixth graders and junior high students could delve more deeply into operations with positive and negative numbers.

OTHER 0–99 CHART ACTIVITIES

To involve younger children with the 0–99 chart, you can have them make 0–99 puzzles. Each child needs a 10-inch square of tagboard, a marker, a pair of scissors, and a small envelope. Each makes a 0–99 chart on the tagboard. You may need to provide the children with tagboard that has the lines already ruled for the chart. If so, you may have to make a smaller chart, one you can reproduce on a 8½-inch-by-11-inch tag, using a ditto machine. However, it is valuable for the students to write the numbers on their own charts.

Children then cut their charts into ten pieces, cutting only on the lines. They write their names on the back of each piece of their puzzles and on their envelopes. After making sure they can put their pieces back together into the 0–99 chart, they put the puzzle pieces in their envelopes. Keep all the envelopes in one place. Students try each other's puzzles, writing their names on the envelope of each puzzle they solve.

Having older students search for patterns on the 0–99 chart is effective for cooperative group work and is also a way to incorporate writing in the math class. (Recent educational articles have focused on the importance of giving students the opportunity to express their thoughts in writing in all subject areas.) It is useful to have calculators available for students as they explore these patterns.

1. What rule or shortcut method can you describe for finding the sum of any three horizontally adjacent numbers? Explain why your rule works.
2. As in number 1, what rule can you describe for finding the sum of any three vertically adjacent numbers? Explain why your rule works.
3. Find a shortcut method for finding the sum of any two-by-two array of numbers. Do the same for any three-by-three array. How are you doing this? Use what you discovered to find the sum of the full ten-by-ten array.
4. Describe a rule for finding the sum of any three diagonally adjacent numbers. Does your rule work for numbers on the diagonal in either direction? Explain.
5. Can you extend your rule to four diagonally adjacent numbers? Five? Describe a general rule.

C H A P T E R

• **6** •

EXPLORING
MULTIPLICATION
WITH
RECTANGLES

• GRADE 4 •

"Take twelve tiles and arrange them into a rectangle."

The children in this fourth-grade class had spent a good deal of time studying multiplication. They knew their multiplication tables fairly well, and most could multiply by a one-digit multiplier with and without regrouping. They had learned that multiplication is related to addition. In response to being asked what multiplication can accomplish, one student said, "It's a way to do adding when you need to add the same thing over and over." Also, they had had experience solving word problems for which multiplication was required.

In this lesson the students investigate multiplication from a different approach — through a geometric investigation of rectangular arrays. Having children look at multiplication from a geometric perspective contributes to their concept development. Too often children's multiplication instruction focuses heavily on learning the rules and procedures for performing multiplication calculations at the expense of learning underlying concepts. Teaching for mathematical understanding must emphasize underlying concepts along with procedures.

When students are learning a new concept, it is helpful to relate that concept to several different areas of mathematics and to involve the students in activities in those areas. None of the students in this class had discovered that the multiplication chart they had been studying could be generated from a geometry investigation of rectangles. Also, none of them had explored visually the patterns of multiples on the multiplication chart. Making these connections was not only enjoyable, it also contributed to their seeing the interrelatedness of the different areas of mathematics.

This lesson spanned five days of instruction in the classroom, and sparked some students to continue further. During all of the activities presented, the children worked in small cooperative groups.

DAY ONE: MAKING THE RECTANGLES

For this part of the lesson, I used one-inch square tiles, paper ruled into one-half-inch squares, and scissors. The children were seated in small groups; there were six groups of four children each and one group of three. I had enough tiles so that I could give twenty-five to each group, and I had duplicated enough paper so that each group had four sheets. I put an extra stack of paper on the supply table. There were enough scissors so each student could have a pair.

I began by introducing rectangular arrays. I explained, "There are twenty-five tiles for your group. I'd like you to work with partners for this first task." I had the students work in pairs because I didn't have enough tiles for each student to have twelve, which they would need for this activity. The class began to buzz as the children organized themselves into partners. Becky's hand shot up. She was in the group of three students; I told them they should work together as a group.

When the students were settled again, I continued, "I want you and your partner to take twelve tiles and arrange them into a rectangle. Your rectangle should be all filled in. Don't use the tiles just to outline a rectangle."

After a minute or so, everyone had accomplished the task. I drew their attention to the rectangles they had built. "Look at your group's rectangles. Raise your hands if both the rectangles are the same." About a third of the children raised their hands.

I continued, "Now raise your hands if the rectangles are different." Again, about a third of the students raised their hands.

"How come some of you didn't raise your hand for one or the other?" I asked.

Peter raised his hand to respond, "I wasn't sure if ours was the same. It looks like the same shape, but theirs is sideways and uses different colors."

Several others nodded to indicate that they were confused about what I meant by rectangles that were the same and rectangles that were different. I continued by asking Peter a question, "I can't see your rectangle from where I am. How could you describe it to me so I would know what you have built. I'm not concerned about the colors, just the shape."

Peter and Jason, his partner, answered together, "It has 4 across one way and 3 across the other."

"Does that description fit your rectangle?" I asked the two others in their group. They nodded yes.

Abby raised her hand. "Ours is different. It has 6 across and 2 down."

"Before we talk about your rectangle, Abby, let's talk a bit more about Peter and Jason's rectangle. Who else in the class built a rectangle that is 4 by 3?" About half the students raised their hands.

I drew a 4-by-3 rectangle on the board, making it 4 squares across the bottom and 3 squares tall. I wrote a 12 in it. "What does the 12 mean?" I asked.

"That's how many tiles we had to use," Sarah answered.

"What if I drew it this way?" I asked, drawing a rectangle with the same dimensions, but positioned so it was 4 tall and 3 across. "Are these two rectangles the same shape?"

Andy answered, "Yes, but one's sideways."

"Yes," I said, "I drew them in different positions, but they have the same dimensions. Both are 3 squares by 4 squares, and we'll consider them the same rectangles. So I don't need both of them. One will do." I erased the second rectangle I had drawn.

I then returned to Abby. "Describe your rectangle again, Abby. What are its dimensions?" Introducing a word which may be new for some of the students, such as *dimensions,* is no problem when done in the context of an activity, especially where the children have a physical model to refer to. Abby answered easily, "Ours is 6 across and 2 down."

I drew a 6-by-2 rectangle on the board and wrote a 12 inside. "Is it OK to write a 12 inside this one also?" I asked. Nods confirmed their agreement.

"How many of you built a rectangle with dimensions 6 by 2?" I asked. About half the students raised their hands.

"Did anyone build a rectangle with twelve tiles that has a different shape from either I've drawn on the board?" I asked.

There were no volunteers, so I offered another possibility. "What about a long skinny rectangle?" I asked, and drew a 1-by-12 rectangle on the board. There were several "Oh, yeah," murmurs. I wrote a 12 in that rectangle as well.

"Let's try another number," I said. "This time work together as a group instead of with partners. See if you can find all the ways to build rectangles with sixteen tiles. Draw each rectangle you find on the squared paper, write a 16 inside, and cut it out. If you finish that and others are still working, do the same for the number 7." I wrote the numbers 16 and 7 on the board.

The groups got busy. It was interesting to watch and notice that finding the rectangles wasn't obvious to them. Generally, groups counted out the sixteen tiles and then started to arrange them. Most groups found the 8-by-2 and the long, skinny 16-by-1 rectangles and then went on to try 7.

One group of four raised their hands. "Does a 4-by-4 square count?" Diane asked.

"Yes," I answered, "a square is also a rectangle, but a special kind. What makes it special?"

Todd answered, "The sides are all the same."

"Then it counts?" Andrea asked, wanting to be sure.

"Yes, because a square is a rectangle, it also counts," I answered. I don't think Andrea believed or was comfortable with the idea that a square could also be a rectangle, and I suspected this was true for many of the other students as well. I had purposely chosen 16 because I planned to discuss this idea with the class.

As I left the group, I heard Diane turn to the group next to them and hiss, "See, I told you it would count."

I interrupted the students as soon as I noticed that all groups had cut out rectangles for 16 and two groups had done one for 7 as well. I called the students to attention and said, "I'll draw on the board what I see you have cut out for the number 16." I drew three rectangles: a 1 by 16, a 2 by 8, and a 4 by 4. I explained to the entire class, as I had to the smaller group, that the square was included because squares were a special kind of rectangle. Also, I wrote 16 in each rectangle and asked the students to check to make sure they had done so. Several had forgotten.

Manny raised his hand, "We did 7 too."

"What did you find?" I asked.

"We only found one, a 1 by 7," he replied. I drew this on the board and labeled it.

"Do you think there are others for 7?" I asked.

"Nope, we think that's it," Manny said confidently.

"I think you have the idea about finding rectangles," I said to the class. "Now I'll explain what your group task is. You are to work together to find all the different rectangles there are for each of the numbers from 1 to 25. Use the tiles to help. Draw each rectangle you find on the squared paper, write the number on it, and cut it out.

"You'll need to find some way to keep organized because you'll be cutting out lots of rectangles. Try to conserve paper by drawing rectangles close to each other. If you need extra paper, however, there's a stack on the supply table. Also, don't forget about the number 12. We already did that one, and the rectangles are on the board, but you'll need to cut them out also. Any questions?"

Andy raised his hand. "What if the paper isn't long enough to cut out a rectangle?"

"Does someone have an idea about what to do then?" I asked.

Robert answered, "You could tape paper together."

"Would that help?" I asked Andy. He nodded, and I added, "I'll put my scotch tape on the supply table as well. Don't take it to your group. Take what you need, and leave it there so others can find it."

"Before we start," I said, "who can tell me what you need to be doing in your group?" I asked this to check that they understood the task and to have the opportunity to clarify any details. I had several of the children respond, encouraging the others to listen and to ask questions if they weren't sure what had been said.

I ended with an additional reminder, "Take a few minutes first to discuss how you will get organized in your groups. Remember, I'll come and help whenever all of you in your group have the same question."

There were no other questions, and the class got to work.

BEGINNING THE WORK TIME

Groups organized themselves in different ways. Some assigned specific jobs so that one student, for example, drew the rectangles and another cut them out. Some groups divided into partners again, each pair taking different numbers. Some split up so individuals tackled different numbers. Some groups stayed together. In general, the children seemed to feel that there was a lot to do in this task, and they responded by settling down and getting busy.

As I wandered and observed, I gave suggestions and reminders to some of the groups. To a group that had a pile of unlabeled rectangles, "Don't forget to write the number of squares on each rectangle." To a group in which each was working on different numbers, "How are you keeping track of which ones you've finished? Can you find a way to check with each other to make sure you've found all the rectangles for each number?" To a group that had a mess of paper on their desks and on the floor, "I see some of your rectangles on the floor. How about taking a minute to get organized. Throw away the scraps, collect your rectangles, and then get back to work."

One group called me over to tell me what they had discovered. Manny explained, "The odd numbers only have one rectangle each."

"Which ones have you done already?" I asked.

They showed me the rectangles they had cut out for 1, 3, 5, 7, 9, and 11. Betsy added another to the pile that she had just cut out, a 1-by-13 rectangle.

"You've come to a hasty conclusion," I told them. "Watch how I can arrange nine tiles into a 3-by-3 square." I did this, and they groaned.

I made one more comment before leaving the group, "I agree that some odd numbers can be done in only one way, but look carefully before you leave a number."

When it was near the time for math class to end and for the students to go to lunch, I put a legal-size letter envelope at each table and interrupted the groups. "It's almost time to stop now," I said. "I'd like you to put your names on your envelope and put all the rectangles you've cut out inside it. Put all the extra paper, including parts of pieces that are still big enough to use for more rectangles, on the supply table. The tiles go in the box on the table, and put your envelope on the table too. Tomorrow, when it's time for math, get your envelope, some tiles, and paper and continue your work."

DAY TWO: CONTINUING THE WORK TIME AND BEGINNING TO SUMMARIZE

The group with Jason, Peter, Stacey, and Robert finished first the next day. I gave them the job of taping their rectangles on the board so we could use them for a class discussion. I numbered across the board from 1 to 25 and asked them to tape each rectangle under the correct number.

As a few other groups finished, I asked them to organize their rectangles by number and to compare what they had found with what was being posted to see if they were missing any or if any were missing from the board. The squares were missed by several groups, as was the 3-by-7 rectangle. Some negotiations went on at this time, and groups worked to fill in what they were missing.

Some groups were taking longer to cut out the rectangles. I let them continue to work and gave groups that were done a worksheet on which I had written questions that related to the rectangles. I had duplicated one worksheet for each group and planned to discuss these questions with the entire class when all groups had finished. Having the worksheets ready gave me a way to deal with the groups that had worked more quickly.

The questions on the worksheet directed groups to investigate patterns:

1. Which rectangles have a side with two squares on them? Write the numbers from smallest to largest.
2. Which rectangles have a side with three squares on them? Write the numbers from smallest to largest.
3. Do the same for rectangles with four squares on a side.
4. Do the same for rectangles with five squares on a side.
5. Which numbers have rectangles that are squares? List them from smallest to largest. How many squares would there be in the next larger square you could make?
6. What is the smallest number that has two different rectangles? Three different rectangles? Four?
7. Which numbers have only one rectangle? List them from smallest to largest.

A group that finished early posts their rectangles for the class.

By the end of class, all but one group had finished cutting out rectangles. I left the rectangles posted on the board for the next day's lesson and directed the students to clean up as before. And I arranged with the group that had not yet finished to have some extra time to finish before math class began the next day.

DAY THREE: SUMMARIZING AND MAKING THE MULTIPLICATION TABLE

I began the next day's lesson by having the students come up to the board so they could more easily see the rectangles posted. Some sat on the floor; others brought up their chairs; some perched on desk tops. I find it easier to focus the class for discussions when the students are together at the front of the room.

First I asked them to report how they had worked on the task in their groups. Though I didn't spend much time on this, I feel it is valuable for groups to share their methods of working. Learning how to organize to work cooperatively improves when students pay regular attention to the processes.

Then I went through each of the questions on the worksheet, listing the answers on the board, discussing the patterns, giving new vocabulary when appropriate. For the rectangles that had a side with two squares on them, for example, Sarah called out the numbers and I wrote them: 2, 4, 6, 8, 10, 12, 14, 16, 18, 20, 22, 24.

"They skip every other one," Robert said, noticing the pattern on the numbers from 1 to 25.

"Who could continue the numbers in this pattern?" I asked.

Betsy volunteered and continued to recite the 2s. I stopped her at 40.

"These numbers are called the multiples of two," I explained, "because each can be written as two times something. Take 2, for instance. It is 2 times 1. 4 is 2 times 2. What about 6? 8?" And I continued this pattern, in order, up to 12.

Then I skipped some numbers. "What about 16?" They answered in unison, familiar with that multiplication fact.

We explored the multiples of 3, 4, and 5 in the same way.

Then we looked at the squares and listed these numbers: 1, 4, 9, 16, 25. They had not initially included the 1 by 1, but agreed that it should be included when I pointed it out to them. "These numbers have a pretty obvious name," I said. "They are called square numbers. The smallest is 1 by 1, next is 2 by 2, next is 3 by 3, and so on. What is the next square number after 25?"

Diane raised her hand and gave the answer 36. I asked her to explain how she had gotten that. "Because 25 is 5 times 5, and next comes 6 times 6, which is 36." I asked them what came next, and as they told me, I continued the list of square numbers to 100.

We located the smallest numbers with two, three, and four different rectangles. They were 4, 12, and 24. "Is there a number that has five rectangles?" Peter asked. I told the class that I knew there was at least one and that I'd leave that problem for those who were interested.

We then listed the numbers that had only one rectangle: 1, 2, 3, 5, 7, 11, 13, 17, 19, 23. I gave the class the mathematical name for these numbers. "Just as the numbers with squares have a name, these numbers have a name also. They're called prime numbers, except that the number 1 is not included as a prime number."

"Why not?" Jason asked.

"One is different from all the other numbers on the list in a particular way," I explained. "Each of the others can be written as a multiplication sentence with two different factors — 2 is 2×1, 3 is 3×1, 5 is 5×1, and so on. But 1 has only one factor, the number 1, 1×1. The mathematical definition of prime numbers is that they have exactly two factors."

"That's dumb," Andrea said.

"Not necessarily dumb," I said, "but perhaps picky. Lots of things in life are arbitrary like this, such as putting the fork on the left side of the plate or always celebrating Thanksgiving on a Thursday. Arbitrary decisions can help us keep things orderly."

I then left that discussion and introduced a way to transfer their rectangles numerically to a chart. I kept the students at the front of the room for this so they could see more easily as I modeled what I wanted them to do.

"Here's what you'll do next," I began. "I'll demonstrate on the board; then you'll each do this individually. You'll each need your own clean sheet of squared paper, but you'll share your group's rectangles."

I taped a piece of squared paper on the board for my demonstration and untaped the three rectangles for the number 12. I took the 4-by-3 rectangle first and placed it on my squared paper in the upper left-hand corner. Then I lifted the lower right-hand corner of the rectangle, explaining what I was doing, and in the square under that corner, wrote the number 12.

I removed the rectangle and explained why I had done this, "If I drew a rectangle around the 12, I would outline the 3-by-4 rectangle I used to locate the 12." The students were watching carefully.

I continued, "Now I'll use the same rectangle, but in the other position." I placed the rectangle in the corner again, and again lifted the lower right-hand corner, writing 12 in the square underneath. I did the same for the 2-by-6 and the 1-by-12 rectangles, writing 12 in four additional squares.

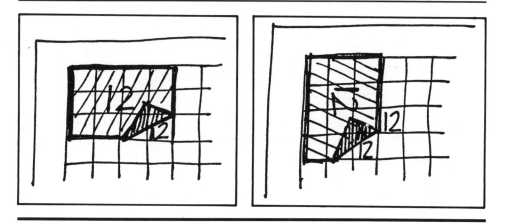

Then I demonstrated the process again, this time using the two rectangles for the number 9. I chose 9 so I could show that for the squares, such as 3 by 3, rotating it doesn't matter since the lower right-hand corner will be over the same square either way.

I then had the students return to their seats and follow this process for each of their rectangles that would fit on the squared paper. I gave them the rest of the class period to finish and told them we would discuss what they had done the next day.

DAY FOUR: INVESTIGATING PATTERNS ON THE MULTIPLICATION TABLE

It wasn't obvious at first to the students that they were constructing part of the multiplication table through this activity. As they worked, some noticed and others did not. However, once we looked at the chart and ex-

1	2	3	4	5	6	7	8	9	10	11	12	13	14	15	16
2	4	6	8	10	12	14	16	18	20	22	24				
3	6	9	12	15	18	21	24								
4	8	12	16	20	24										
5	10	15	20	25											
6	12	18	24												
7	14	21													
8	16	24													
9	18														
10	20														
11	22														
12	24														
13															
14															

The cut-out rectangles produce part of the multiplication table.

tended the patterns, it became clear to the students that this was the multiplication chart they were familiar with, that the numbers they were writing were products.

It was exciting to watch this happen because of the students' excitement. So often children learn math without understanding the basis for what they are learning. This connection of the numbers in the multiplication table to the rectangles was an eye-opener for many of them.

We discussed the patterns in what they had done. We looked at rows with patterns that were familiar to them—the 2s, 5s, and 10s. I modeled for them how we could continue those rows as far as the sheet allowed. Then we did the same for the 2, 5, and 10 columns.

We then tried the 3s. Some knew the multiples. I showed them how to "skip count." Also, I had them check their numbers with a calculator, showing them how pressing 3, then +, then = repeatedly would display the multiples of 3.

I left them to complete their multiplication tables so at least a 12-by-12 array of numbers was filled in.

"When you have filled in your tables," I also explained, "I want you to look for patterns. I'd like you to write the patterns you find on a strip of paper." I had cut some plain white paper into three-inch-by-eleven-inch strips. "Then we can post them and compare."

On the 9's starting with 9 going down on the last number of the number it goes 1 lower.

In the 6 column or row, if you add the digits in the product you get the pattern 6, 3, 9, 6, 3, 9...

On our multiplication table, for the 10's × n just add a zero to that number and you have the answer.

Every thing in the 11's column is double digit.

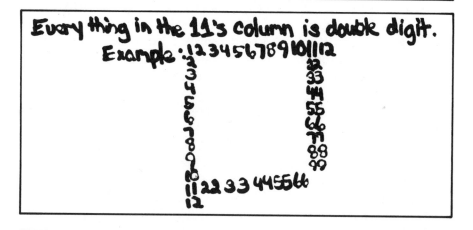

Students describe patterns from the multiplication table.

They found a variety of patterns.

Everything in the 11's column is double digit.

On our multiplication table, for the 10's × n just add a zero to that number and you have the answer.

On our table, if you multiply the number at the top of a column by a number at the left of a row, the product will be where the row and column intersect.

On the even numbered rows or columns, all of the products are an even number.

On the odd numbered columns and rows, the products are odd, even, odd, even, odd, even.

On our multiplication table for the nines, the product will add up to nine.

On the 12 column, for 1 × 12, 2 × 12, 3 × 12, 4 × 12, the answer will have a 1, 2, 3, or 4 in it.

On the fives if you start at the bottom of the column on the last number of the number it goes like 0, 5, 0, 5, 0, 5, etc.

If you look at the square numbers on our table, the number just above and just to the left are the same.

In the 6 column or row, if you add the digits in the product you get the pattern 6, 3, 9, 6, 3, 9 . . .

On our table, the difference between our square numbers increased by two each time.

DAY FIVE: FURTHER EXPLORATIONS ON THE MULTIPLICATION TABLE

For this day's activity I duplicated a stack of multiplication tables, enough so there were eleven for each group. In this experience, the students would be examining visual patterns on the multiplication chart. I explained to the children what they were to do.

"I'm going to show you another way to investigate patterns on the multiplication table," I began. "I call these Times-Table Plaids. I'll demonstrate with the multiples of 6. First I need to make a list of the multiples of 6. Read them to me from the 6 row or column on your multiplication table." As the children read the multiples, I wrote them down the side on one of the multiplication tables I had duplicated. The list went to 72.

"What is the largest number on the 12-by-12 table?" I asked.

They answered, "144."

"We need to continue the list of multiples to get as close to 144 as we can. We can add 6 to 72 to get the next number. What is that?"

After a moment, Sarah gave the answer, "78."

"We could continue adding 6, or we could use a calculator," I said. "You can choose either method. Do you think we'll land on 144? Is 144 a multiple of 6?"

Most of the children had no idea. Jason thought so, but wasn't sure about his explanation, "I think so, because 144 is in the 12s column and so is 6."

We continued the list. Jason was pleased to find that he was correct, that 144 is a multiple of 6.

"Once you have your list of multiples made," I continued, "you need to color in all those multiples on the multiplication table." I demonstrated, starting with 6, coloring in the four different squares in which it appears and then checking it off. Then I went to 12 and colored in the six squares in which it was written and checked it off.

"You can continue in this way," I said, "or you may find a pattern that helps you see what to color. Any questions so far?"

There was none, so I continued. "As a group, you are to complete eleven charts — for the multiples of 2, 3, 4, 5, 6, 7, 8, 9, 10, 11, and 12. Decide who will do which numbers, but be sure that you each do different ones. Look at the patterns that emerge. We'll post a set and talk about them later as a class."

1	2	3	4	5	6	7	8	9	10	11	12
2	4	6	8	10	12	14	16	18	20	22	24
3	6	9	12	15	18	21	24	27	30	33	36
4	8	12	16	20	24	28	32	36	40	44	48
5	10	15	20	25	30	35	40	45	50	55	60
6	12	18	24	30	36	42	48	54	60	66	72
7	14	21	28	35	42	49	56	63	70	77	84
8	16	24	32	40	48	56	64	72	80	88	96
9	18	27	36	45	54	63	72	81	90	99	108
10	20	30	40	50	60	70	80	90	100	110	120
11	22	33	44	55	66	77	88	99	110	121	132
12	24	36	48	60	72	84	96	108	120	132	144

Patterns emerge when multiples of numbers are shaded.

When the class got to work, I wrote the numbers from 2 to 12 on the board, leaving room so a colored-in chart could be posted beneath each number. As children finished charts, I asked them to tape the charts to the board, so that soon one of each had been posted.

We had about fifteen minutes at the end of class for discussion. "What did you notice?" I asked.

Andrea raised her hand. "The 2s surprised me," she said. "I thought it would look like a checkerboard, but it was in stripes."

Manny's hand was raised. "Some just have stripes, but some have stuff inside the stripes." Others had noticed that also.

"Which of the numbers have just stripes?" I asked.

We picked them out together — 2, 3, 5, 7, and 11. "Who remembers the special name for these numbers?" I asked.

Several children raised their hands. "They're prime," Peter said.

"We colored in multiples of only two square numbers," I said, "4 and 9. Do you notice anything about them?" The 4s pattern has a pattern of one square inside each larger square of stripes; the 9s pattern has a pattern of four squares in it.

The children talked about other things they had noticed. Though they saw patterns, it was difficult for them to describe in words what they saw. This is not uncommon, and it is with this practice of trying to verbalize what they see that they will improve.

I kept the posted tables for a bulletin board display on which I had children post also the patterns they had written the day before.

IN CONCLUSION

The children enjoyed the explorations. Though such an experience will not result in their memorizing multiplication facts, children develop a familiarity with multiples, deepen their understanding of the concept of multiplication, and have the opportunity to see relationships between numbers and geometry. The week was well spent.

Abby reads for her group, "If Billy wants six pencils and five erasers, how much more money does he need?"

CHAPTER ·7·

BILLY AND THE PENCILS

· GRADE 4 ·

Children's experiences with word problems are too often unsuccessful ones. The usual procedure is for students to be assigned a page of word problems that appears in their text. If the word problems on the page follow a lesson in a particular operation and simply require applying that operation, students may not have too much difficulty. If, however, the problems on a page require a mixture of operations or if they call for using several operations in one problem or if they contain extraneous information, many students are at a loss.

"Do I need to add or subtract?" is not an uncommon question for students to ask teachers. Arriving at answers that make no sense when considered in the context of the problem is not unusual. When approaching word problems, students more often wonder What do I do to get the answer? rather than How can I make sense out of the situation?

Assigning students word problems to solve does little more than test their abilities to solve the word problems. Such assignments are not learning opportunities. They provide reinforcement and practice for students who already know how to solve the problems. However, they offer frustration to students who don't know, contributing to their feeling of powerlessness and their negativity toward learning mathematics.

This lesson was conducted in a fourth-grade class and describes one approach to helping students make sense of word problems. In the lesson the students are told to focus on what can be asked from a typical word-problem situation, rather than concentrate on how to get the answer. This activity is only one of many that can help students in this area of their math study.

PRESENTING THE SITUATION

I began the lesson by organizing the students into small groups to maximize their opportunity to collaborate in their thinking and to benefit from each other's ideas. There were seven groups in the class—one with five students and six with four.

Once the children were settled in their groups, I wrote the following on the chalkboard:

> Pencils cost two for $.25.
> Erasers cost $.10 each.
> Billy has $1.00.

I explained to the students what I wanted them to do. "There are three parts to the directions I'm going to give you now," I told the students. "I'll tell you what they are, and then I'll write them on the board so you won't have to remember them.

"The first part is this," I continued. "I'd like each of you, individually, to write one question that can be answered from the information about pencils, erasers, and Billy. Then comes the second part. When you have written one question, I want you to read your questions aloud in your groups. After each question is read, discuss as a group whether it can be answered from the information given. After that, you'll go on to the third part. Working together, think of as many questions as you can that can be answered from the same information. Collect your groups' questions on one sheet of paper. You may or may not include the questions you wrote individually first. That is up to your group to decide."

I then wrote the directions on the board, getting the students to contribute by recalling what I had said, and answered questions as each direction was written.

1. By yourself, write a question that can be answered from the information posted.

2. In your groups, read your questions aloud, discussing whether they can be answered.

3. In your groups, brainstorm as many questions as you can that can be answered from the same information. Write them on one sheet.

The students got to work. For a few minutes, as students wrote their own questions, the room was quiet. Then as students began to read their questions to each other and to brainstorm other questions, it became noisier. Still, it was possible for all the groups to work, and none seemed disturbed. Purposeful noise, such as the sound of children working together, never seems to be a deterrent to productive work.

PROCESSING THE QUESTIONS

After fifteen minutes or so, I interrupted the students. I had noticed that there were at least six questions on each group's list, which was sufficient for the next activity. I told the children what it was I'd like them to do next.

"I'm going to have the groups share the questions you've written. Here's how we're going to do that. Each group, in turn, will have the chance to read a question. In a moment I'll give you a chance to decide who in your group will do the reading. Also, you'll have to decide which of your questions you'd like to read."

Then I asked a question: "Do you think it's possible that when we have gone around the class once, with each group reading a question, that we'll have heard seven different questions?"

From the number of nods and murmurs, I could see they thought it was certainly possible.

"Why are you so sure?" I asked.

Todd raised his hand. "We have some really great questions on our list," he said.

"So do we," said Becky.

"Do you think we'll be able to go around the room twice and still have each group ask different questions?" I asked.

Some of the groups still felt confident. Others weren't so sure.

"We'll try it and see," I said. "But this means that along with reading your question, you'll have to listen carefully to the others to make sure that you aren't reading the same question. And sometimes questions can really be the same though the exact wording will be different.

"I'll give you a few moments to decide who will do the reading for your group and to decide on the questions you plan to read. It will be a good idea to have a backup question in case yours has been read."

I structured the activity this way to encourage them to listen to each other. Too often students are very willing to offer their thoughts, but have difficulty listening to each other's ideas. Giving them a reason to do so, such as not reading the same question, helps them focus when others are speaking.

I explained the order of the groups for the first round and made one additional comment, "We won't worry about actually finding answers to the questions now, but I want you to think about whether it is possible to answer each of the questions read from the information."

Abby began by reading for her group, "If Billy wants six pencils and five erasers, how much more money does he need?"

"Can that be answered from the information?" I asked.

"Yes, I can figure it out," Robert said.

"So can I," said Terry.

"I'm not interested in answers right now," I reminded them. "I'm interested in hearing the different questions you wrote."

Robert read next for his group, "How many pencils and erasers can Billy buy for $1.00 and not get any change back?"

"How about that?" I asked. "Can that be answered?"

Some students nodded, but I realized that without having time to actually try to solve the problem, most were not sure if it could be done. I decided not to continue asking if questions could be answered. Instead, I would focus on whether what was asked was a new question. I didn't announce this decision to the class, but acted on it after the next question was read.

Andrea read next, "If Billy has $1.00 and he already bought two pencils, how many erasers can he buy?"

"Is this question different from the others?" I asked and was answered with nods. I called on the next group.

Diane read, "Billy has to give his friend Fred $.25 because Billy borrowed it. But Billy's teacher said that he needed five pencils by tomorrow. Will Billy have enough money to buy the pencils and pay Fred back?"

The class seemed impressed with this one.

Peter went next. "How much does one pencil cost?" he read.

Abby raised her hand. "We didn't put that one on our list because we didn't think you could answer it," she said.

"Yes, you could," Peter answered. "If you went into a store to buy one pencil, the store owner wouldn't send you away. He'd sell you a pencil."

Robert chimed in, "But you can't tell for sure how much he would charge for it."

"I think it would be $.13," Sara offered. "That's as close to half as he could get, and he'd charge the extra half cent because he had to break up a pair."

"But you couldn't know for sure," Abby insisted.

"Is the question different from the questions that have been asked so far?" I interjected.

My question was answered with nods.

"Let's leave it for now," I said, "and you'll have a chance to argue about how to answer it later. Who will read next?"

Manny read next, and he was very excited about their question, "If Billy bought one pencil and three erasers plus two more pencils and said to the clerk, 'Forget the half of a cent,' how much does Billy get back?"

Andy offers to explain when Peter challenges the question Stacey read.

Stacey read for the last group, "If Billy pays $1.00 for one eraser and two pencils, how much change will he get? Then if he sells each one for $.02 more, what is his profit?" Stacey was visibly pleased with her group's question. However, her face took on a look of dismay when her question was challenged.

"That's not one question," Peter said. "You asked two questions. That's not right."

"I know how to fix it," said Andy, who was in Stacey's group. "Just give me a minute."

We waited patiently while Andy scribbled. Then he read, "If Billy has $1.00 and buys one eraser and two pencils and then sells each one for $.02 more, how much money does he have now?" He looked at Peter and asked, "Is that OK?" Peter nodded.

"So," I said, "it seems we went around the room and heard seven different questions. Could we make another round? Would you like to try?" The students were enthusiastically willing.

I gave the groups a chance to look over their lists again. I also changed the order in which the groups would read.

We started with Diane this time. She read, "Billy has a little sister who

Group 2

1. If Billy buys 5 erasers how many pencils can he buy?

2. If Billy buys 4 pencils and 2 erasers and Billy gives the clerk $1.00 how much change will he get back?

3. If Billy bought 6 pencils how many erasers could he get and what would be the amount of change he gets back?

4. If Billy bought 1 pencil and 3 erasers plus 3 more pencils and said to the clerk "forget the half a cent!" How much does Billy get back?

5. If Billy bought 6 pencils and 2 erasers how much change does he get back?

6. If Billy bought 4 pencils and 5 erasers how much change does Billy

---

In their fourth question, this group solves the problem of what to do if someone purchases only one pencil.

Group 3

1. If Billy has $1.00 and he already bought 2 pencils, how many Erasers can he buy?

2. If Billy bought 5 Erasers and 2 pencils will he get any change? And if he does how much will he get back?

3. How many Erasers and pencils can Billy buy, the number has to be the same? What is the least amount of change he can get back?

4. If Billy gave his friend .15 cents, how many pencils can he buy?

5. Billy thought he could buy 20 pencils. (He didn't know how much they cost) How much did he think they were?

Group 3 was especially proud of their fifth question.

needs two pencils and two erasers. Billy needs four pencils and two erasers. Does this cost more or less than $1.00 and how much change will Billy get if he gets any?" The class agreed this was a different question.

Peter read next, "How many erasers and pencils can Billy buy if the number of each has to be the same?" This question interested me, maybe because it was a question I don't think I would ever have thought of myself. (The uniqueness of children's thinking is part of what makes teaching fascinating to me.) I was becoming curious about what the students would do when asked to solve these problems, but I continued the activity with the class.

Manny and his group needed a minute to scan their list again. Finally Manny read, "If Billy bought six pencils and two erasers, how much change does he get back?"

Stacey went next, "How many erasers can Billy buy and have $.10 as change?"

Then Abby, "If Billy pays $1.00 and gets $.20 back, how many pencils and erasers did he buy?"

Robert then read, "Billy thought he could buy twenty pencils. He didn't know how much they cost. How much did he think they were?"

And finally Andrea again, "If Billy bought four pencils with tax of $.03 on each, how much would he pay?"

"Would it be fair," I asked the class, "if I gave you the assignment of solving the fourteen questions that have been asked about Billy and the pencils and erasers?"

The students indicated that they thought this would be fair.

"Would you rather solve them alone or in your groups?" I asked.

The answer was unanimously in favor of working in groups. "You learn just as much," Andrea said, "or even more from helping each other."

"Let me explain what I want you to do," I went on. "For homework tonight I want you to solve the problems your group wrote. Solve all of them, not just the ones you read. You'll do this individually. I'll give you time in a moment to copy them. Then tomorrow, in your groups, you'll compare your answers to the problems."

EXTENDING THE ACTIVITY

I planned to use these problems during the next several days, and I had several different ideas for doing so. I would begin the next class by having the students compare the results of their homework problems and resolve any discrepancies. Then I wanted them to focus on the two questions they had read aloud yesterday. Each group would write their agreed-upon answers for those two problems, putting each answer on a different sheet of paper. I wanted those two sheets of paper handed in for me to correct. My goal was to have fourteen corrected sheets in an answer folder to be available later to the students.

Next I wanted groups to write each of the two questions they read on a large sheet of drawing paper, using wide markers, so that they could be posted for everyone in the class to see. I would then number the problems, for convenience, and structure activities using them.

For starters I wanted to provide an experience from which the children would be alerted to the fact that in some problem situations there is more than one possible answer. Too often children quickly come to a conclusion and then stop thinking, rather than investigate the situation further. The activity I planned for the students, in groups, was to sort the posted questions into two groups—those that had only one possible answer—How much change did Billy get?—and those that had more than one possible answer—What could Billy buy with $1.00? As a class, we would discuss how they sorted the questions.

Then I wanted the groups to find solutions for the problems. They could work on them in any order. When they believed they had one solved, they would check their answer against the solution in the answer folder. If their answer conflicted with the answer in the folder, they were to check with that group to resolve the difference of opinion. I would step in if they couldn't come to an agreement.

Other experiences are necessary also to help students focus on making sense out of word-problems. Such experiences include the following:

1. Students write word problems for different equations. Start by giving the class the same equation, perhaps a simple addition sentence, such as $8+6=14$. Ask each student to write a story for the equation that meets two criteria—it ends in a question and the question can be answered by the equation. Students read their stories to each other in their groups. Those who are willing read them aloud to the entire class.
2. Students choose their own equations and write stories for them following the same two criteria. They read their stories aloud in their groups so others can figure out the equation. These can be posted and used as a class assignment for matching equations to situations.
3. Students write stories for equations, but this time include extra information that isn't needed. It's best to model this type of story for the students first. For example: Sally was planning a birthday party. She mailed nine invitations. Seven friends replied that they could come. Sally went shopping for refreshments with $10.00. She bought a cake mix for $2.69, three six-packs of soft drinks for $1.19 each, and a sack of chips for $1.29. The day before the party one of the guests who had planned to come phoned to say she had an unexpected visit from her grandparents. How many guests attended the party?
4. Using a page of word problems from the textbook, students, in groups, decide for each whether in real life an exact answer is needed or if an estimate will suffice or is perhaps even better. They have to explain their reasoning.

5. Using a page of word problems that you know requires a mixture of operations, ask the students not to solve the problems, but to decide whether they will need to add, subtract, multiply, or divide, or some combination of these, in order to find an answer.

6. Each student brings in a label from a can of food or an empty box and writes word problems that could be answered from the information on the label or box. Students solve each other's problems.

It is after a series of activities such as these that I would have students tackle word problems from their text. I want to observe if by that time they are focusing on making sense of the situations. I would still have them discuss their answers together rather than work alone on assignments. It's only when I need to assess their individual abilities to solve word problems that I have them work independently. Thus, both they and I can find out what they understand. In classroom lessons, however, I'm interested in establishing a classroom environment that focuses on learning to think and reason, not on testing what they were supposed to have already learned.

Playing cards are useful for organizing students into groups of four.

CHAPTER

·8·

THE CONSECUTIVE SUMS PROBLEM

• GRADE 5 •

Helping children develop the ability to apply their mathematics knowledge to problem-solving situations is a general goal of elementary math teachers. Students need experiences that require them to use higher-order thinking skills. They need to be challenged to use their math skills in new situations in which they make and test predictions, analyze patterns and relationships, organize information, and formulate generalizations.

Another important goal is helping children develop a positive attitude toward mathematics. A positive attitude is more than finding math experiences enjoyable. It includes feeling a sense of power and satisfaction at having successfully tackled a mathematical problem. It includes feeling that the problem was mathematically interesting. A positive experience leaves students open and eager for more math.

This lesson, conducted with fifth graders, responds to both goals. It required that students apply mathematics skills they have learned—finding addends for sums up to 35. It required that students apply those skills to a new situation—they were to find all the ways to write numbers to 35 as the sums of consecutive addends.

The students were organized into small groups and asked to work cooperatively on the problem. It was the first time students in the class had been asked to work in this way. The benefit of working cooperatively quickly becomes obvious to the students as they explore what is required for this problem.

Also, this lesson models for the teacher the benefits of having students work cooperatively. Because students in small groups discuss what they are doing, the teacher has the opportunity to hear how the students think, observe how they interact with each other when facing a problem, and see how they choose to organize and record their work.

PRESENTING THE PROBLEM

There were twenty-one of the twenty-four fifth-grade students in the class the day I taught this lesson. I had an hour and a half to work with them. After introducing myself, I explained what I would like them to do.

"I am going to give you a mathematics problem to work on this afternoon. Before the end of class, I'll be interested in hearing what you enjoyed about solving the problem, what you didn't enjoy, what you learned, and any other reactions you had. Your sharing can help me learn about what makes sense to teach.

"Before I tell you about the problem, I'd like to explain how you'll be organized. I'm going to put you into small groups to work so that you won't have to solve the problem alone."

The students' desks were in traditional rows and had to be rearranged in order to form groups. I decided to put the twenty-one children into six groups, three groups with four students in each and three groups with three students in each. Also, I wanted to group the children randomly and had playing cards to do so. I took all four aces, 2s, and 3s along with three of the 4s, 5s, and 6s from a deck and shuffled them.

I explained all this to the students and told them that we would first rearrange their desks; then I'd assign seats. "For this lesson you may not be sitting in your regular desk," I told them. I asked, "Will this be a problem for anyone?" No one responded, so I continued.

I directed the students to move their desks into the six groups, and then I numbered each cluster—ace, 2, 3, 4, 5, 6. I asked the children to come up in an orderly line so each could choose a card from me to find where to sit. "You'll be needing something to write with," I added, "so please bring that with you when you come up to pick a card."

Getting them seated into their groups took a little more than five minutes. When they were settled, I wrote "consecutive numbers" on the board and began by asking a question. "Do you know what consecutive numbers are?" I asked. Several hands went up. I chose Nelson to answer. "They go in a row," he offered, and others nodded.

"Are 23, 24, and 25 consecutive?" I asked. In response I got nods. "What about 59, 60, 61?" More nods. I was doing this to focus them on me as much as to check their understanding. "How about 42, 43, 46?" Head shakes. "How about 14, 16, 18?" This caused some head nods along with shakes.

Lisl explained, "They aren't consecutive because they skip numbers."

Peter added, "You could say they are consecutive even numbers."

I agreed with both of them and told them that in this problem, we would be dealing only with consecutive numbers that differ by one. I posed a part of the problem they would be asked to solve. I wrote a 9 on the board and asked, "How can you write 9 as the sum of consecutive addends?"

I gave the class a few moments to think even though several hands immediately shot up. Then I called on Tracy. "Four plus 5," she responded, and I wrote that on the board.

"Can anyone think of another way to write 9 as the sum of consecutive addends?" I asked. This time I called on Seth. "Eight and 1," he said and quickly corrected himself by adding, "That won't work — they're not consecutive."

I had written $8 + 1$ on the board when Seth offered it, and now, before erasing it, I asked the class, "Do you agree with Seth that this isn't correct?" There was general agreement.

After a few more moments, Akiko raised her hand and blurted out at the same time, "Two plus 3 plus 4." I wrote that on the board, and the class murmured agreement.

"Any other ways?" I asked again. After some silence, I continued with the class.

"Let's leave that for a moment. You'll have a chance to think more about it when you're working on the whole problem. What you are to do in your groups is to investigate all the numbers from 1 to 35 and find all the ways you can to represent each as the sum of consecutive addends. Before you start, let me give you some guidelines.

"First of all, I'll give each group one sheet of paper on which I'd like you to record. How you organize the paper and who does the recording are group decisions you'll need to make. I would like each of your names at the top, however, along with your group number.

"Next, be warned that some of the numbers cannot be written as the sum of consecutive addends. There is a pattern to them, however, so that when you find the pattern, you can use it to predict all the numbers that are impossible.

"Some of the numbers can be written only one way, and there is a pattern to those numbers as well. There will be other patterns you may notice as you work. I'll be asking you about them later.

"As you're working, one rule that I will follow is that I will come and help you only when everyone in your group has the same question, so you'll need to discuss all that you're doing.

"Remember, you are to find all the possible ways to write each of the numbers as the sum of consecutive addends. What questions do you have?"

I had given the class a great deal of information and realized that it was important that they have the chance to ask any questions they might have. Thus, some of the directions will be clarified, and others will be restated in different ways. Still, I know that not all the students will be clear on what is expected of them. Having them in small cooperative groups helps enormously in this situation because the children will pool their knowledge and clarify their task together.

Several questions were raised. "You mean we can write our answers any way we want?" "How high do we need to go?" "Can we use scratch paper?" "How do we decide who does the writing?" "What if we don't find all the ways?" I answered all questions at this time.

Marcie asked, "Do we use 0?"

I directed my answer to the entire class. "It's up to your group to decide whether or not you want to include 0. You'll need to investigate to see if 0 changes the patterns you notice."

Once all the questions were answered, I asked them to get to work.

DURING THE EXPLORATION

As I circulated, I noticed that groups got started differently. Several were engaged in discussion, heads together, spending time deciding how to organize before they started looking for consecutive addends.

One of those groups began by focusing on the recording. Karine suggested, "Let's number the paper from 1 to 35." "I'll do it," Marcie said. "That's good," Seth commented, "my writing isn't too good." "But I don't want to just write," Marcie continued. "I want to find some answers too." "You can," Karine said, "because we can save the ones we find on scratch paper, and then every so often you can put them on the chart." And so they went to work, Marcie organizing the chart, Seth and Karine looking for consecutive sums in no particular order.

Another group wasn't at all concerned with the chart, but focused on organizing who was going to look for what. Jonathan made the initial suggestion, "Let's divide up the numbers so we're each looking for something else." The group accepted that suggestion, and they decided that with 35 numbers, they would each have 8, but there were 3 extras. "The person with the smaller numbers should have more," Mark said, thinking that the larger numbers would be harder or more work. So they agreed that Lisl

Marcie organizes the chart while Seth and Karine look for sums.

would do 1 to 10, Akiko would do 11 to 19, Mark would do 20 to 27, and Jonathan 28 to 35.

Other groups did not give this initial time to organizing. One group of three did not talk to each other at all; instead, each student went to work independently, looking for sums on separate pieces of paper. I watched them for a while and finally asked them how they were organizing their effort. They looked up, seeming almost surprised at being interrupted. "You're each working hard, it seems," I commented, "but I notice that your group chart is empty. How do you plan to collaborate on that?" They looked at each other for a few moments. Finally Scott said, "When we each have done all we can, we could compare." Peter nodded. "Not yet, though," Jessica said, adding that she needed more time. "It seems you are comfortable working this way," I said, "but pay attention to the time so that you'll have your chart done before the end of the class." They nodded and immediately fell back to working individually.

Another group decided to work together, searching for consecutive addends for numbers sequentially. Amy was recording. They called me over fairly soon after they had started. They had gotten to the number 7, having found solutions only for the odd numbers. Their chart looked like this:

1 = 0 + 1
2 = impossible
3 = 1 + 2
4 = impossible
5 = 2 + 3
6 = impossible
7 = 3 + 4

"See," Amanda said, "we've already figured out the pattern. All the even numbers are impossible." Kathy, Amy, and Doug nodded in agreement. It is not unusual for children to come to generalizations quickly and invest totally in them before looking more deeply. When such thinking is incorrect, my way of handling the situation is to provide a contradiction that allows them to see that they need to look further. "Do you agree that the numbers 1, 2, and 3 are consecutive?" I asked. They nodded. "How much is 1 plus 2 plus 3?" I asked. "Oh, no," Amy groaned, "that shoots our theory," and she began to erase "impossible" after the 6. "What is the pattern?" Amanda asked, feeling discouraged. "I'd rather not tell you that; I want to give you the chance to find out," I answered and left when they went back to work.

Several times individual students came up to me with a question. In each of those instances, I would accompany the student back to the group and have the question stated again for the group. In all but one of those instances, the group answered the question without my intervening, and in each instance I reminded the students to check with each other before seeking my help.

One group had a question that had them all stumped. They had found consecutive addends for many of the numbers, had decided that 2, 4, 8, 16, and 32 were impossible, but were disturbed because they couldn't find consecutive addends for some of the sums here and there, and they were frustrated. I spent a bit of time getting them to focus on other patterns that might be helpful. I told them what David had shared with me (he was not in this group), and together we checked the sums with three addends. Starting with 0 + 1 + 2, the sums went up by 3s—3, 6, 9, 12, 15, 18, and so on. They saw immediately that the pattern could be helpful, and though it added another alternative in a few places, it didn't help with any of the holes on their chart. "What about looking at four addends and seeing if there is a pattern there," I suggested. They got started, and Kathy verbalized what they were finding, "First 0 + 1 + 2 + 3 = 6, then comes 1 + 2 + 3 + 4, and that's 10, and 2 + 3 + 4 + 5 is [after a pause] 14." Jason got very excited, "Look, it goes by 4s, and that takes care of 22. We found one for 22." I left them to continue working.

During this time, two groups came to me to announce that they were done, asking what should they do next. Each group had found one way to write each number and more than one way to write only some of them. I wanted them to search further, and in each instance I pointed out another direction. "I notice that you don't have any with four addends. Let's try one together. How much is $1 + 2 + 3 + 4$?" After the mandatory fifth-grade groan, they added that one to their chart and were willing to keep looking for others.

SUMMARIZING THE EXPERIENCE

I asked the students to stop work so that I would have twenty minutes left for a class discussion. They weren't all finished, and I realized it, but for this first experience, I decided that I wanted to spend some time in class discussion, then give them the chance in their next math period to continue and extend their investigation.

First I asked them to report how they had gotten organized. I wanted the students to hear the different ways groups approached the problem, thereby reinforcing the idea that different ways are acceptable. I wanted to stress that it is important to choose a procedure that is useful for the task. Some groups reported that they had changed their methods while they were working. The group that was approaching the numbers in sequence realized that their procedure wasn't very efficient since they were finding solutions for other numbers and didn't want to "waste" them. They then extended their chart so they would be able to add whatever they found. The group that had divided up the numbers so carefully found that they began to help each other with their numbers and wound up collaborating together more than they had planned.

I asked them to report how they had decided who would do the recording. A ripple of laughter went through the class. In most groups it was just one person who grabbed the chart or one who was given the job. Generally, very little discussion had contributed to making this decision. One girl complained that she would have liked to have written. I said that she needed to tell her group and pointed out that groups needed to listen and to be sensitive to each other.

I then focused on the patterns they were noticing. "How many groups figured out the pattern of the impossible numbers?" I asked. All hands went up. "I'd like to hear how you would describe the pattern," I continued. Several raised their hands, and I had each of them give a description, each time asking if someone could explain it in a different way. "They double." "They are all times 2." "See, you take one and then you add it to itself and you get the next one and you keep doing that." "They go by 2s."

I was interested in seeing if I could get them to express the generalization more clearly and told them I'd like to write a statement on the board that describes the pattern. "What should I write?" I asked. This was very difficult for them. Though they knew what they meant, they had difficulty expressing themselves. We worked as a class on the statement for a bit. I didn't push it very far, sensing their difficulty and realizing that they needed a good deal more experience expressing their ideas.

As a final question, I asked them for reactions to the lesson—what they had enjoyed and hadn't enjoyed, how they felt about the group work, what had been difficult and what had been easy, what they had learned. Their reactions were positive. Amy's comment was a tribute to the potential of cooperative groups, "Everyone could do something, even if you're not that good in math, and that was good."

I told them what I had observed, pointing out the strengths I had noticed and those areas in which I thought they needed more work. I told them that I felt they worked well together, but told them they seemed more interested in getting the answers and getting done instead of searching for the patterns. I told them that I thought they would get better at looking at the mathematics when they had more experience. I told them that I felt they were doing interesting thinking, but that it seemed hard for them to explain their thinking, and that we'd work more on the explanations in the future. And I told them I had enjoyed their enthusiasm and how well they stuck to the task.

The lesson was a good beginning.

Which letter occurs most often?

a
e
s

"This rolled-up strip of adding-machine tape shows the letters of the alphabet in order of their usage."

The order of usage of the letters of the alphabet is useful, even essential, information for some people. Manufacturers of bulletin board letters, marquee letters, and artists' press-type letters certainly need to know. Though computers have replaced most hand typesetting, the order of usage is essential for manufacturers of wooden or metal type. The order of usage is also valuable to people who break codes, important at times for our national security, and recreational at times for those who solve puzzles such as cryptograms. Inventors of games such as Scrabble and Boggle need to consider the order of usage when they make decisions about the scoring and about how many of each letter will be available.

In this lesson fifth graders are engaged in a statistical study in which they investigate the order of usage of the letters in the alphabet. Students are introduced to several concepts in the area of statistics during the lesson. Each student chooses a sentence and finds out how often the letters of the alphabet occur, an activity that requires collecting and organizing data, skills basic to the study of statistics. Students compare their individual data with the data collected in their groups and then with the data collected in the entire class, giving them experience comparing results from different sample sizes. Students interpret their data to make inferences about the actual order of usage of the letters. Finally, their inferences are compared to the statistics available from analyses made of much larger samples.

The exploration also gives students practice applying arithmetic skills to a problem situation. Too often students learn and practice arithmetic skills yet do not always see the connection between these skills and situations that arise in the world. Getting the right answer, rather than using the answer, is too often seen as most important. In this activity students use the answers to their calculations to come to a decision about the alphabet. Also, this investigation presents the students with a mathematics problem that is connected to a real-world situation.

The lesson was conducted over two days. Follow-up ideas that extend the exploration are also given.

PRESENTING THE ACTIVITY

"For the next few days," I announced to the fifth graders, "we'll be studying the alphabet. You'll be involved in a math exploration with the alphabet in a way that helps you investigate ideas about probability and statistics.

"You'll be doing your work in small groups," I went on, "but first I want you each to make an individual prediction." The students were used to working in groups of four, with groups of three or five when the number in attendance demanded. They were also accustomed to individual assignments.

I described the prediction I wanted them to make. "Without discussing your thoughts with any of your group members, predict what you think are the five most commonly used letters in the English language, the letters that occur most often when people write books, newspaper articles, magazine articles, whatever. List your choice of five letters and put a star next to the one letter you think is used most."

I gave them time to make their individual predictions. Having students consider a situation independently before having a group discussion is useful. It gives them a chance to formulate their thinking. Then the group discussions provide opportunities for them to explain their thinking, get responses to their ideas, and hear and respond to others. The group process gives students perspective on their thoughts and helps them clarify, extend, and change what they have been thinking.

INTRODUCING A GROUP ACTIVITY

After the students had had time to make their individual predictions, I explained what they were to do in their groups. "Share your predictions in your group and come to a group decision about what you think are the five most commonly used letters and which one occurs most."

During this time of group discussion, I enjoyed circulating and listening to their interaction. Groups differed in how they arrived at their conclusions. Some groups opted for the majority-rule principle, deciding that because three of the four students had a common opinion, it became the group's final decision. Other groups had a particularly strong personality in them and deferred to that person's power. One group negotiated by giving each of the members a piece of the decision, taking *a* from one person's list, *n* from another's, and so on. Having groups report the methods they use for coming to a group decision supports the understanding that there is more than one way to think about a problem, and that encourages flexibility in thinking.

I wrote the groups' predictions on the board. *A* was chosen by all but one of the groups as the letter that would occur most often. On all lists there were more vowels than consonants. I asked them why this was so. Jessica's explanation was that because all words had vowels, they were bound to be used more frequently. The class agreed, and no one offered another idea. *S, t, n,* and *l* were the consonants that appeared most often on their lists.

REAL-WORLD CONTEXTS

I then took some time to link the question to the world outside the classroom. I raised a question for class discussion: "Who in the world would care about the order of usage of the letters of the alphabet? Can you think of anyone who needs to know or who would benefit from knowing?" A few hands went up after a minute, but most of the students remained still.

After a bit I called on Peter. "No one would care," he said. The class tittered.

"Not so," I answered. "I know of several instances where this information would be very useful."

Karine's hand shot up, and her face became very animated. I asked her what she was thinking. "That show on TV where you get to guess letters to make words. They could guess better if they knew which letters were used most." This made sense to the class, and even Peter acknowledged it as a reasonable response to my question.

"Any other ideas?" I asked.

"Scrabble," Jonathan offered.

"How does the usage of the letters affect Scrabble?" I asked.

Jonathan wasn't sure, but Amy contributed that some letters are worth more than others and that there are more of some letters than others.

Through more discussion, they recalled that *a* and *e* were worth only one point while *q* and *z* and *x* were worth a lot more.

"I have another use," I told them, "which doesn't have to do with a game, but with a manufacturing problem." I showed them a sheet of press-type letters I had bought at an art store, the kind of type that you transfer onto paper by rubbing. "This type is commonly used by artists and designers when they need lettering," I explained. I showed them how a letter was transferred onto paper and explained further, "The alphabet appears twice, once for upper case and once for lower case. But the number of each of the letters differs. These sheets wouldn't sell very successfully if artists ran out after a sentence or two."

"See," said Marcie who was sitting near the front, "there are more *a*'s and *e*'s and not so many of others."

INTRODUCING THE SAMPLING ACTIVITY

I then told the class that I actually knew which letter was most common and, as a matter of fact, I had already prepared a list of all twenty-six letters of the alphabet in order of their usage in the English language. "I've written this sequence on a strip of adding-machine tape," I explained, showing them the strip rolled up and secured with a paper clip. I tacked the strip, still rolled up, above the chalkboard. "Before unrolling it, however," I told them, "we are going to conduct a mathematical investigation. You will take statistical samples, and we'll use the information you gather to predict the order of usage of all twenty-six letters of the alphabet. Then we'll check our prediction with what is on the rolled-up strip."

I wasn't troubled that the students didn't know what statistical samples were. I was going to describe the activity, and they were going to actually do it. By the end of the lesson, they would have had the concrete experience of collecting and interpreting statistical samples, and the abstraction would take on some reality.

"It would be very difficult," I continued, "to take all the writings ever done in the English language and count up how many *a*'s were used and how many *b*'s, *c*'s, and so on, but we can look at smaller samples. I'd like each of you to do the following for homework tonight. Pick a sentence with at least five words in it from any book. Copy the sentence onto a piece of paper. Find out and record how many times each letter of the alphabet appears in your sentence. Bring your recording sheet tomorrow to use in your group."

A homework assignment such as this has several characteristics that distinguish it from the more usual assignments for skill practice. First of all, though the assignment defines a task to be done, the students have flexibility in how they will approach it. In this way students are given a problem-solving rather than a practice assignment. Second, the homework won't be handed in to be corrected by the teacher. Instead, it will be used for further

THE PRIME MERIDIAN OF LONGITUDE passes through the town of Greenwich, England.

brian

The size of land and ...

b i.
2 1

Scott

What according to the article, are some clues that people from the past have left for us.

a	b	c	d	e	f
3	0	4	1	10	3

g	h	i	j	k	l
1	5	2	0	0	4

m	n	o	p	q	r
1	8	4	3	0	5

s	t	u	v	w	x
4	9	1	1	1	0

y	z
0	0

Students use different approaches for organizing their homework.

investigations in their groups, giving the students the opportunity to see in the next class period the usefulness of their efforts.

REPORTING INDIVIDUAL SAMPLES

When the students reconvened for math the next day, I started the class by having individuals report how they had done their homework. Amy showed her work. She explained that she had listed the alphabet and then had worked through her sentence, making a tally mark next to the letter in her list for each letter in the sentence. As she had made each tally, she had crossed out that letter to keep her place. When she had finished, she had written the number of times each letter appeared after each set of tally marks. *E* had come up most often, occurring twelve times. Second in line had been *n*, with six tallies, followed by *g, h, i, r,* and *t,* each with five tallies.

Scott had used a different method. He also had listed the letters of the alphabet, but instead of going through the sentence, letter by letter, as Amy had done, he had started by counting all the *a*'s in the sentence, then searching and counting all the *b*'s and continuing through the sentence that way. *E* also had come out most often, occurring ten times; *a* had occurred eight times and had come in second; *t* was next with nine occurrences. Scott, however, had not used a system such as Amy's crossing out each letter, to insure that he had counted all the letters.

Brian's method differed from the other two. The sentence Brian had chosen began with the word *The.* He had started with *T,* the first letter in his sentence, and had counted all the *t*'s, crossing them out as he did so. He then had gone on to *h* and had counted those, again crossing them out. Then he had done the *e*'s, continuing through the sentence until all letters had been crossed out. In Brian's sample, *e* and *n* had occurred most often, both the same number of times.

Other methods reported were variations on these three. The students' work reinforced for me the benefit of giving students the responsibility for organizing themselves rather than giving them a dittoed worksheet. Creating worksheets gives the teacher practice organizing information on paper, but doesn't help students get better at it. Making students responsible for organizing their recording for a particular task gives them valuable experience.

COLLECTING THE GROUP DATA

I then gave the students a group task. "You need to compile your records to find group totals for how often each letter appeared. I'll put a large class chart on the board, and when your group is finished, one of you should enter how many times each letter of the alphabet appeared in all of your sentences combined." The chart looked like the following:

a b c d e f g h i j k l m n o p q r s t u v w x y z

Group 1

Group 2

Group 3

Group 4

Group 5

Group 6

TOTALS

I continued with additional instructions. "If you have extra time before all the groups have entered their data on the chart, I have two additional activities for you to try." I posted them for the students.

1. Discuss in your group what is unusual about the four sentences below:

> THIS IS ODD. DO YOU KNOW WHY?
> TRY AND FIND OUT. GOOD LUCK!

2. Play the You Can't Say *L* game. One person starts to talk, trying not to say any word with the letter *l* in it. Others in the group listen. When the person talking uses a word with an *l* someone else tries.

When all the groups' data were entered on the chart, I went around the room assigning four or five letters to each group so we could find the class totals. The students had calculators to use for this task. I told the students I thought it best if several people did the totals for each letter as a check on our statistics. Using the calculators as a tool in this way makes sense to me. I'd use it if it were my task, and I think children need to learn to use tools that adults depend on.

There was a great deal of scurrying in the room as children figured totals, checked them, and entered them on the class chart. Finally all the totals were entered. I had all the students pull their chairs up to the front of the room to be closer to the class chart. Together we used the group chart to list the letters in their order of frequency from our samples. As the children identified them, I wrote the letters in sequence on the chalkboard below where I had taped the listing on the adding machine tape. That way I could unroll my tape and we could compare the two.

Before I unrolled the tape, I asked them what they thought would happen. This was a good time to probe their thinking. I certainly had their attention for the big moment. No one thought the class order would exactly match the order on the tape. I asked them whether they thought more than half or less than half would match. Opinions varied. I asked them how much of the order would have to match for them to be satisfied with our statistical sample. I asked them what would disappoint them. I didn't expect them to have firm notions about these questions, but I wanted to raise them as beginning ideas for understanding the use of statistical samples.

Students record their group's statistics on the class chart.

Finally, while Mark gave a good imitation of a trumpet call, I unrolled the tape. Their eyes widened. The first eight letters on both lists matched, though two letters differed in order. And even though some of the rest of the letters were in different order, the similarity of the two lists was impressive to them.

DISCUSSING AND EXTENDING THE INVESTIGATION

We continued to talk about the investigation. I raised several questions, more for discussion than for coming to conclusions. What would happen if we had done a larger sample? How might the results differ if we had used first-grade readers instead of the assortment of books we did use? What if we used sentences from a book written in Spanish or French or some other language? If we were to try the sampling experiment again, would we be likely to produce results that would match exactly the order on the adding machine tape? Why do they think mathematicians say that larger samples will more closely resemble what really happens? Do they think a larger sampling of letters would produce results closer to the actual order?

I told them what I had learned about the typewriter keyboard. When Christopher Sholes invented the typewriter in 1867, he purposely scrambled the letters so that typists couldn't type too quickly and jam the letters. That was before the invention of electric typewriters, which eliminated the problem of jamming when someone typed quickly. On a typewriter keyboard, more than half of the strokes are done with the left hand, the weaker hand for most people. The two most agile fingers on the right hand rest on j and k, which are two of the least used letters. The left pinky, the weakest finger for most, rests on the a. In 1930 August Dvorak designed a keyboard on which it is possible to type more quickly. Although used on some Apple computers, it has not received widespread use.

Next I asked that they do an extension assignment. They were to choose one of the following activities.

1. Design a typewriter keyboard that makes use of the results of our mathematical experiment. When you have finished, you will be able to compare it with the Dvorak keyboard.
2. Investigate the game of Scrabble. List the letters in the game two ways — in order of their values and in order of how many there are of each. See how it relates to our findings. Describe your thoughts as to why you do or do not think the Scrabble scoring or the numbers of each letter ought to be changed.
3. Do a statistical sample for another language and compare the results with our findings for English. If others in the class choose this assignment, combine your findings for a larger sample.
4. Cryptograms are communications written in code, in which each letter stands for another letter in the alphabet. Whichever letter is used as a substitute for a, for example, is used for a throughout the puzzle. Figure out this message:

AB CD EDDF AG FXD HIJY
A CAKK LMN NZM IG AWD WJDIE WZGD.

Here's a clue: the most frequently used words in the English language are *the*, *an*, *a*, and *and*.

The unit was successful in several ways. It's not necessary that students in the elementary grades understand all the aspects of statistical sampling. It is useful, however, for them to experience some of these ideas now as a basis for their later learning. Many aspects of our adult lives are shaped by statistical samples: insurance rates are a prime example. Our representation in government or allocation of certain government funding also relies on statistical samples.

The group organization made it possible even for the students who have difficulty learning to get the help they needed to participate. The extensions allowed for a variety of follow-ups. It was interesting and useful for me to observe which activities had appeal for which students. And it was nice to relate mathematics to another subject and situations outside school. Too often math exists in isolation as a study unrelated to the world.

The order of usage of the letters is as follows: ETAONISRHLD CUPFMWYBGVKQXJZ. (Those bracketed have the same frequency of occurrence.)

The Dvorak keyboard organizes the letters as shown in the illustration.

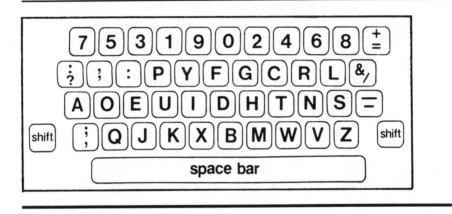

CHAPTER

·**10**·

FOOT

ACTIVITIES

• GRADE 5 •

Kathy and Melissa work together to trace their foot outlines.

A sequence of lessons is presented in this chapter, each lesson involving the students with measurement activities using their feet. The lessons were conducted in the same fifth-grade classroom on four different days spread over a two-week period.

There were several purposes to the activities. One was to give students experience with area in ways that differed from their usual focus on applying formulas to regular shapes. A second purpose was for students to study the concepts of area and perimeter in relationship to each other rather than as separate topics. A third was to provide a context in which students could investigate finding averages, using the data they generated from their foot areas. And all the students' learning was to occur through problem-solving experiences in which the students were expected to think and reason.

Between the presentation of the first foot activity and the second, the students explored area and perimeter through four additional activities. Those activities gave the students the opportunity to explore the relationship between the area and perimeter of shapes in several contexts and with several different materials.

The benefit of having students interact with a concept through a collection of varied experiences is that the concept doesn't get tied to a specific situation. Instead, students' learning is developed from a broader experience of interacting with the concept in a variety of ways. In this approach students have the opportunity to connect each new experience to what they have already learned, which both cements their understanding and extends it.

Students were asked to write in connection with each of these activities, both to describe what they had done and to explain their thinking. This was not something the students were used to doing in math class. Their usual experience was to complete an assignment and be done with it, rather than reflect and think further about it. Most of their first efforts were not satisfactory. However, with attention and persistence, their writing improved and their thought processes deepened. It was worth the effort.

FIGURING FOOT AREA

For the first experience in this sequence of lessons, I wanted the students to figure the area, in square centimeters, of one of their feet and to write a description of how they did it. I had dittoed a supply of squared centimeter paper and showed a sheet to the class.

"This is squared centimeter paper," I began and asked, "Who can explain why this is called squared centimeter paper?"

Almost half the class volunteered. I called on Lisl. "It's in squares, and the lines are a centimeter apart." Others nodded in agreement. I continued with my introduction.

"For this activity," I explained, "you'll each figure out the area of one of your feet. You'll use a sheet of squared centimeter paper to do this. There are three parts to the activity."

I placed a sheet of the squared paper on a short stool in front of the class, took off my left shoe, and placed my foot on the paper. "For the first part of this activity, you'll need to place one foot, with your shoe off, on the paper and carefully trace around it to get an outline of your foot." As I talked, I outlined my foot with a pencil. "It helps to be careful and to hold the pencil vertically so you get an outline that is as accurate as possible. You might find it easier to work with a partner and trace each other's foot. Any questions so far?"

There weren't any. I added one comment, "This is not hard to do, but it does tickle just a bit if your feet are sensitive." This was to avoid giggly reactions when they got started. (I had already heard several teasing murmurs about taking their shoes off, which I chose to ignore.)

I continued, "For the second part of this activity, you have to figure out the area of your foot, which means to find out how many square centimeters your foot covers. You'll notice that there will be bits and pieces to think about since your foot doesn't totally cover all squares, and you'll need to decide how to account for them. Your answer won't be completely accurate. That would be very difficult, even impossible, with a shape as irregular as your foot. But I'd like you to come to as close an approximation as you can. What questions do you have about this part before I tell you the last part?"

Mark raised his hand. "Can we mark on our feet?" There was a burst of laughter in response from the class. Mark went on, "I didn't mean on my feet. I meant on the drawing of my foot."

"Yes," I answered, "you can mark on your foot drawing any way that is helpful for you."

I called on Melissa. "Can we work together on this?" she asked.

"You can work with a partner to get a tracing of your foot if you like," I responded, "but I want you to work independently to figure your area. I'm interested in your individual thinking and work on this problem."

"Does it matter which foot we outline?" David asked.

"Either foot is fine," I answered.

There were no further questions, so I explained the third part of the activity to them. "When you have figured the area of your foot, I want you to write an explanation that describes how you did it. Write on the lined paper and hand it in with your foot. Be sure to write your name on each sheet."

Before having them get started, I decided it was a good idea to write the three parts of the activity on the board, as it was a lot for some of them to remember. A written reference is essential for some students and helpful for all. It also gave me the chance to show them how to write an abbreviation for square centimeters. I wrote:

1. Trace around one foot (shoe off) on squared centimeter paper.
2. Figure the area of your foot in sq. cm.
3. Write a description of how you did this.

My final direction was that those who completed the task before the others were to continue on their social studies project after they had handed in their work.

The students got busy. As I circulated and observed, I noticed that students were working basically in two different ways, though with some variations. Some were partitioning their feet into squares and rectangles, finding the areas of those, then dealing with the leftover pieces. Others were counting all the whole squares inside their foot outlines one by one, some numbering each one as they counted, some coloring in all the whole squares, some marking them with an X or other mark. One child drew a rectangle that enclosed her foot, figured its area, then worked to figure out how much she needed to subtract.

Tracy was one of the few students who raised their hands for help. Her question was a usual one for her and no surprise to me. "Am I doing this right?" she asked.

"Tell me what you're doing," I responded.

"I'm counting the whole squares first, and then I'm matching up the extra pieces to see which fit together to make more wholes," Tracy explained.

"Do you feel your method will help you find out how many square centimeters there are in your foot?" I asked.

"I think so," Tracy said, "but I want to make sure."

"Your method makes sense to me," I told Tracy. "There are other ways as well to do this, and we'll have the chance to find out later what different methods were used by others in the class."

Several other students raised the same sort of question. I try to acknowledge the children's need for reassurance yet still make them responsible for their work and decisions. I feel that it is only after they have had sufficient experiences with success that they will move toward more independence.

When I read the students' papers that night, I found a wide variation in their written descriptions. A few were detailed and explained their thinking clearly. More, however, were vague and unexplanatory. Some were garbled and unclear. The following samples are reproduced with the children's misspellings and other errors.

From Nelson: *I figured it out by counting the whole ones. When I was done I tried to put all the uneven squares together. I put the uneven squares together by putting a big uneven square with a small uneven square. 152 squares can fit in my foot.*

From Kathy: *I counted the squres that were hole then I counted the squres that were not and my foot came out to be $120\frac{1}{2}$.*

From Amy: *To find out the area of my foot I traced my foot on centimeter graph paper. I found out that my foot is 112 square cm.*

My method was to make a rectangle around a large group of whole centimeter squares. Then I multiplied the length times the width.

With small pieces of squares I tried to find two pieces that formed a whole. Then I put the number zero in one and the number one in the other. I would count the piece with the one in it.

From Jerry: *The way I got it was I counted what was in the picture of my foot.*

From Marcie: *This is how I found the area in my foot. I put it in rectangles and squares and counted it that way and then added it.*

From Lisl: *The way I got it was by first coloring the whole squares lighter. Then I added half to half and if there was a square that only needed a little corner I would look for one and add them. My total score is 139 sq. cm.*

From Karine: *I started by coloring and adding the "not whole" boxes blue. There were 55. Next I colored and counted the whole boxes yellow.*

Karine

I started by coloring and adding the "not whole" boxes blue. There were 55. Next I colored and counted the whole boxes yellow. There were 92 I then divided 55 by two since the fraction boxes rounded out would be about half. 27 r1 was my answer. I then added 92 and 27 which was 119. I added the remainder 1 because I shouldn't leave out part of the number and the area of my foot was 120 square cm.

Karine decides that all partial squares could be considered approximately one-half of a square.

There were 92. I then divided 55 by two since the fraction boxes rounded out would be about half. 27r1 was my answer. I then added 92 and 27 which was 119. I added the remainder 1 because I shouldn't leave out part of the number and the area of my foot was 120 square cm.

From Jonathan S.: *Step 1 First I colored all of the whole squares brown. I found the number of the brown squares and wrote it down on my paper.*

Step 2 Then I colored the half squares orange. I found the number of half squares and wrote it down.

Step 3 After the halves I did the quarter squares. I colored them green. I wrote down the number and continued.

Step 4 I then colored the three-quarter squares black. I wrote down the number and I added up all of the wholes, halves, quarter, and three quarter squares. My answer was 152³/4.

From Brian: *I counted them with meshment with a ruler.*

I wrote comments on each paper, giving them suggestions about how they might better describe their work. On most I referred them to the work they showed on their papers with their foot outline.

The next day I discussed what I had observed when they were working in class and my reactions to their writing. "When you were working on figuring the areas of your feet yesterday, I noticed a great deal of thinking going on. You were solving the problem in different ways, and I found your

Jessica tries to be as accurate as possible by estimating fractional parts of squares.

methods interesting and effective. Except for Jason and Scott, who were absent, you all finished the activity.

"Last night I looked over your work on your foot outlines and read your descriptions. Some of your descriptions told me both what you had done and what you were thinking. Others, however, did not give me very much information about what you did or what you thought. If I hadn't been in class with you, I wouldn't have much of an idea about the thinking and problem solving you were doing.

"Because this is the first time I've asked you to describe your work in writing, it is a good time for us to discuss writing. I think it's important for you to learn to describe your thinking in writing for several reasons. One is that it makes you rethink what you've done, and in that rethinking you strengthen your own understanding and learning. Another is that your writing can help me better understand how you are thinking, so I can know how to help you continue to learn."

I had decided to read aloud some of the papers to help the children understand what I wanted them to do. I explained this to them: "Without reading your names I'm going to read a few of your descriptions. We'll discuss them together. I believe this will help you think about how you can improve your writing. Then I'll return your papers to you, and you'll see what comments and suggestions I have made to you. Then you'll have a chance to rewrite and improve your descriptions."

I continued, giving them some guidelines for listening when I read. "When you hear the description, I want you to decide whether you get a picture of what the writer is really doing and understand the method used.

When it isn't clear, I'll ask you to think about what could be added to help make it clear. I'll share my thoughts as well."

I began with Nelson's paper. They thought it was a clear description, and I agreed. I then read Kathy's as a contrast, and we talked about the similarity in their methods. I told them that though I understood how the smaller bits of squares were put together in the first description, I didn't have that information in the second. I told them that I needed details in order to understand their thinking. I reinforced how important it was for me to be able to understand how they thought.

I then read Amy's description, and they thought it was very clear. I followed hers with Jerry's and Marcie's papers, and again we discussed what was missing; then I asked them for suggestions.

"Remember," I told them, "that this was just the first time I've asked you to write in math class. I hope you look at this as a learning experience. Because what you think is important to me, I'll be giving you more practice describing your thinking in writing. I think you'll find it will get easier for you."

I concluded the discussion with one more direction. I posted a class list on a large piece of chart paper and asked that they record the area of their feet on it.

I collected their rewrites the next day and found that for most of them their second attempts were indeed better.

From Marcie, for example: *I first drew the biggest rectangle that I could that would fit inside my foot. I figgered out how many squares in my rectangle by multipling the length and the width. I combined smaller pieces together to make more wholes. The total number of whole squares were 105.*

From Brian: *I counted the full squares and then I estamated and put the halfs together and the quarters together. I got 111$\frac{1}{2}$.*

During the next five class periods, the students worked on a collection of other activities that involved them with the concepts of area and perimeter. For those they worked either individually, with partners, or with their groups. They could work on the tasks in any order. I introduced all the tasks at one time and posted each on a piece of chart paper for their reference. The tasks gave them experiences that related to the additional foot activities I had planned.

One of the tasks was called The Perimeter Stays the Same. It is referred to in one of the group's writing for the next activity. In this activity students were asked to draw five different closed shapes on squared centimeter paper, drawing only on the lines on the paper and drawing shapes of which each had a perimeter of exactly thirty centimeters. They were to find the area of each of their shapes. Then they were to cut out two of them, the one with the greatest area and the one with the least area, and post them. I had designated sections labeled Greatest Area and Least Area. I asked the students to notice the difference between these two sets of shapes as they were posted.

Students carefully place the yarn on the outline of the foot drawing.

The other tasks were variations — making shapes with a loop of yarn for the perimeter and investigating their areas, making shapes using tiles, or cutting paper shapes with fixed areas and seeing what different perimeters resulted. It was after this collection of experiences that I returned to their foot outlines for further investigation.

A GROUP-OF-FOUR INVESTIGATION OF FOOT AREA

I prepared a problem for the students to work on in groups of four. I told them that in their groups they were to evaluate a method used by a student to figure foot area. I told them that this wasn't a method reported by anyone in their class. I explained the problem to them and then gave each group the problem in writing as shown.

Foot Measuring

To do the assignment of figuring out the area of one foot, a student in the class wanted to avoid counting squares and bits of squares. The student reported the following method: "I cut a piece of string equal to the perimeter of my foot. I did this by

As a group we discovered
that the students method didn't
work.
   We took a peice of string
equal to the perimeter of
Kasara foot. Then made
the string into a square
on graph-papper and counted
the squares inside.
With the first method Kasara
used she got $137 cm^2$ with
the students method she got
$170 cm^2$.

Amanda, Kasara, Brian
and Jerry

This group comes to their conclusion from investigating just one of their group member's foot measurement.

carefully placing string on the outline of my foot. Then I re-shaped this string into a square and figured out the area of the square. This is how I got my answer."

As a group, discuss this student's method for figuring foot area. Write a group report (1) stating whether you do or do not think the method is a good one, and (2) explain your reasoning.

I returned their outlined feet to them and put out string, scissors, tape, and more squared centimeter paper. I suggested that they use the tape to anchor their string when shaping it into a square.

This was the first time I had tried this particular activity with a class. I learned from the trial that I should have been specific that the students try the activity with their own feet. Most of the groups tested the method using just one person's foot, which made for too much looking on by some of the group members while others worked with the string. Also, I would rather they make generalizations from more than one specific instance.

nelson, Karine, akiko, Kathy

If you have two shapes that are different, but have the same perimeter the area inside both shapes doesn't have to be the same.

After investigating the problem, this group reports a generalization.

Some students were disturbed because their string didn't make a square that exactly enclosed whole centimeter squares. I think I would rewrite that direction to read: Then I reshaped this string as close to a square shape as I could so that it enclosed only whole squares.

Conclusions from three of the groups differed from the conclusions of the other three. Three groups reported that the method wasn't a good one because it didn't work for their one trial. Their explanation was based on their experience, with no further explanation or conjecture.

From Amanda, Kasara, Brian, and Jerry: *As a group we discovered that the students method didn't work. We took a peice of string equal to the perimeter of Kasara foot. Then made the string into a square on graphpapper and counted the squares inside. With the first method Kasara used she got 137 cm^2 with the students method she got 170 cm^2.*

From Peter, Jason, and Jon W.: *No, because we counted the area of the foot and it was 128, so that's the right answer. But, using this new method, we got 192, and that is obviously way off.*

From Doug, Lisl, Mark, and Tracy: *We think it is a bad method. For one thing it is hard to get a perfect square. We think it comes out wrong or at least different. When we counted the square area it is different than the foot area but the perimeter is the same. Our yarn stretched a little too.*

The other groups reported their results by presenting broader generalizations.

From Marcie, Amy, David M., and David C.: *Our table disagrees with the person because when the perimeter stays the same it doesn't mean the area stays the same.*

From Nelson, Karine, Akiko, and Kathy: *If you have two shapes that are different, but have the same perimeter the area inside both shapes doesn't have to be the same.*

From Jonathan S., Seth, Melissa, and Jessica: *We do not agree with this method because it gives a too high number. But it is like The Perimeter Stays the Same in the way that if we took a foot perimeter and changed it into a thin rectangle, it will have a lower area than if we changed the perimeter into a thick rectangle or square. In The Perimeter Stays the Same the shapes with the least amount of area were thin. So if we put the foot perimeter into a thin shape the area will be less than what it would be with a thick shape.*

Groups read their reports aloud for a class discussion. Though all the students seemed to learn from the problem, it became clear to me that some of the students did not yet have sufficient understanding or experience to understand the broader generalization reached by others. It is essential that I get information about specific students in this way so I can plan appropriate instructional activities for them.

FINDING THE AVERAGE-SIZE FOOT

It is valuable to relate experiences from different strands of the mathematics curriculum. These children had had some previous experience with averages, and here was an opportunity to use a statistical idea to analyze a measurement activity. Also, this would set the stage for another group-of-four activity using their feet.

I drew the class's attention to the chart on which they had each recorded their foot areas. "Let's take a look at your foot area measurements," I said. What stood out first on the chart was that David C. had changed his foot measurement twice after initially recording, from 136 to 146 to $150\frac{9}{20}$.

"What's the story, David?" I asked. "Has your foot been growing these last several days?"

David is a bright boy, knowledgeable about mathematics and comfortable with abstractions. He is generally invested in being precise, and this was a clear indication of that need.

"When I checked my work the first time, I realized I had added wrong and changed it to 146. Then I did it again and figured the extra pieces more accurately," David explained.

I was perplexed about how to deal with his answer. Coming to an approximation that included $\frac{9}{20}$ of a square centimeter seemed pretty ridiculous to me. But I knew David's tenacity about being exact.

"If you figured it again, do you think you would get exactly $150\frac{9}{20}$ again?" I asked David.

"Yeah, I think so, but maybe not," he answered.

I addressed the entire class, "When I first introduced this activity, I remember telling you that you couldn't really get an exact answer. Can someone explain why I said this?"

I waited, giving the students time to think, and then had several of the students offer their thoughts. They explained, using different words, that you can't really be exact with all those bits of squares that had funny shapes. It is important for students to understand that we sometimes rely on approximations because the constraints of measurement make accuracy impossible.

I finally brought my focus back to David. "So, David," I said, "what would you be satisfied with as a reasonable estimate for the area of your foot if I asked that it be made to the nearest square centimeter or half of a square centimeter?"

"I'd say 150½," he said and came up and changed it once more. Even giving an answer to the nearest half square centimeter seems inappropriate, but since so many of the other students had come to halves in their answers, I thought it was a degree of accuracy consistent with what the other students had used.

I changed the attention now. "Who has the smallest foot area in the class?" I asked.

"I do," Melissa said, giggling. "My foot is only 91 square centimeters."

David M. wears a size twelve shoe. The kids call him Bigfoot, but respectfully so, as I've heard that a stomp from him on the playground is no fun. David said, "Look, mine is 190 square centimeters. That's almost 100 more than Melissa's."

"Is David's foot area more or less than twice Melissa's?" I asked the class. I heard both answers and asked for explanations. It is from incidental opportunities such as this one that children's math concepts can be consistently supported.

David and Melissa came up to the front of the room and put their feet side by side. It was a startling contrast.

"Here's a problem I want you to think about in your groups," I told the class. "Using the information that Melissa's foot area is 91 square centimeters and David's is 190 square centimeters and what you know about your own feet, what do you think will be the average foot area in the class?"

Most groups averaged the two numbers by adding them and dividing by two. Two groups went further, averaging their own feet and then changing the average of David and Melissa's areas to more closely align with their average.

We discussed those answers, and then talked about how we could find the class average. This gave me a chance to explain the difference between mean, median, and mode. To find the median, they lined up in the order of the size of their foot areas and found who was in the middle of the line. There was no mode.

To figure the mean, we talked about the usefulness of calculators, and the students used them to find that the mean was just about 160 square centimeters. They did this in their groups of four and compared answers before reporting. Most found it helpful to work in pairs, with one reading the numbers and the other punching them in, which helped to avoid mistakes.

THE GIANT'S-FOOT PROBLEM

The average foot area was needed for this last activity — to draw a giant's foot, given the information that the area of the giant's foot is just about twice the area of their average foot. Once again they were given an accompanying writing assignment — to describe how they accomplished the task.

I figured out my foot by tracing my first foot, adding in various places, and counting as I went along. When Jessica and I did our first foot it was a disaster. We traced my foot then traced it again right next to it, we attached it then added to the heel. It looked like a Tulip.

by tracy

Tracy describes the initial attempt she and Jessica made to draw the giant's foot.

Also, students were given the option to work alone, with a partner, or with a group. Twenty-two of the twenty-four students were in class that day. Five chose to work alone, ten worked in partners, and there were a group of three and a group of four. About half of the students needed time the next day to finish their work.

The methods the students chose varied. Several used one of their feet as a starting place. Tracy and Jessica began by using Tracy's foot. Because it was just a bit smaller than the class average, they figured that the giant's foot was a little bigger than two of their feet. Tracy wrote: *I figured out my foot by tracing my first foot, adding in various places, and counting as I went along. When Jessica and I did our first foot it was a disaster. We traced my foot then traced it again right next to it, we attached it then added to the heel. It looked like a Tulip.*

They went back to work the next day, deciding to work independently, but then submit one final foot. The final foot was Tracy's idea. She began with her foot again, but proceeded differently this time. Jessica recorded: *The next day we got into an arguement. I tried my own plan but it didn't work. I know how Tracy did hers. First, she copied her foot. Then, she*

Akiko begins her solution by drawing a rectangle with the area of the giant's foot.

added on to it until she got to 260. I think it looks like a giant human foot. She did a very good job!

David M. was a member of the group of four. David is the boy who wears size twelve shoes. They used his shoe for a starting place. Jonathan S. recorded in his usual step-by-step style:

(1) First we took David Master's shoe and outlined it on two peices of graph paper. We did this because David's shoe was the closest to 260 and it would be a good support for the origanal outline.

(2) We all counted the area of his foot drawing. It had an area of 230.

(3) Because it was 30 square cm short we added on to the heel of the drawing.

(4) We copied the foot on another two pieces of graph paper. We counted the area and we got 260 square cm on the dot.

(5) We copied it agian and then we cut it out and taped it on another piece of paper.

(6) Now we rest.

Another common approach was to draw a rectangle about the right size and work from that. Kasara worked alone using this method. *I started off by myself and thought to myself how I was going to do this problem out. I thought if I made a box and then counted the toe space, it would be easyer than counting the hole foot. I thought how long and wide I wanted my foot. I made my foot 31 by 8 which would be 248. I added some on and then counted the rest of the hole square cm. I added 8 + 5 and 248 and got a total number of 261. And thats how I got my strange foot.*

Akiko also worked alone. *First I made a rectangle of 260 boxes. The way I got this rectangl is my multiplying 26 × 10. I made the rectangle a little bigger in case the toes will be wider or taller. I made a shape of a foot. When I counted the boxes it was to big 274. So I cut 14 boxes around the heel, then I got 260. But I didn't really like the shape that much.*

Amanda and Amy began with the same approach, but they made an error at first that caused them a problem. They changed methods, and after three tries they were satisfied. They described their process:

Our job was to draw a foot in which the area was 260 square cm. We thought *it would be EASY. HA!*

Our first try we figured out we should make a rectangle 130 × 20. We thought that would equal 260 cm. We taped six sheets of paper together. Mrs. Scheafer [their teacher] *didn't know what we were doing. Neither did we.*

Our second try we did 30 × 8. We tried to make it look like a foot. We didn't try hard enough.

Our third try was more successful. We just enlarged Amanda's foot 4 sqs out. It actually looked like a foot.

We counted the sqs and they equaled exactly 260 cm.

Other students began by drawing a foot and adjusting it. Lisl, Marcie, and Karine reported their method: *We taped two pieces of paper together to make the rectangle of 300 square cm fit. Then we drew a foot inside. After that we colored all the wholes green and the fractions yellow. Then we counted whole squares and added the fractions. We found out the answer was 250 altogether so we added to the toes and got 257, so we added to the heel and finally got 260.*

Summarizing the activity with the class the second day provided the chance for students to hear each other's methods and compare solutions. The children were curious about each other's drawings and enjoyed sharing their work in this activity. Each posted their giant's foot and came to the front of the room for a presentation. Knowing they will be presenting helps them realize that it is important to be clear and complete in their descriptions.

After each presentation, I asked the other students if they had questions to ask to clarify any part of the description and if they had any comments. Several times the comments began, "We did ours like that, but instead we . . ." In those cases I interrupted the students and asked that they not explain their work yet, but keep their comments to reactions to what had been presented.

After the presentations, I asked a question. "Did anyone think of making a giant's foot that was twice as long and twice as wide as one of yours? Would that be a good idea?" I gave them a moment to discuss it among themselves before I asked for a response. I called on Peter.

"That wouldn't work," he said, "because the foot would be way too big."

Amy chimed in. "First I thought so. But then I realized that if you made it twice as long and twice as wide, you'd be able to fit in four of your feet, not two. It would be four times as big."

Tracy raised her hand. "My tulip foot was the right size, and it was only twice as wide. If I made it twice as long, I'd need to use two more feet."

Having a discussion such as this after the students' concrete experience is a way to help them begin to think about what happens to the area of a shape when you double both its dimensions.

I had one more question for the class. "Suppose we averaged the giant's foot in with your feet. Would that change the class average?" The students all nodded yes. I continued, "Discuss in your groups what you think the new average would be. Think about the mode, median, and mean and how each might change."

I knew this would be a difficult question for many in the class, possibly for two-thirds of the students. Even so, I thought there was value in posing it. In situations such as this one, the more capable students have the chance to explain their thinking to others – a thinking opportunity in which they often clarify their own understanding as they explain.

Also, the other students have the chance to hear an approach to a solution and to observe someone thinking in perhaps a different way from what they had experienced before. Even for students who do not understand totally, the experience can contribute to their math learning. I remind these students, that rather than looking at it as something they don't know, they can see it as something they haven't learned yet. It's this attitude toward learning that I want to be pervasive in the math classroom.

earned $10
earned $20
lost $10
came out even
earned $40
lost $30

Seth, Jonathan, and Kathy act out the horse problem for the class.

In most of their mathematical experiences in school, students are accustomed to doing problems where the correctness of their solutions is verified either by the teacher or by an answer key. Though children are asked to check their work, there is nearly always some authority that is the final judge. They therefore do not learn to rely on their own reasoning to evaluate and justify the correctness of their answers.

This lesson with fifth graders models an antidote. Students are presented with a problem for which the primary focus is kept on their justifying why they think their solutions are reasonable and correct.

The students were organized into small cooperative groups for the beginning of the lesson. Later they were reorganized for part of the lesson so that the students could listen to other solutions and explanations and try to understand the points of view of other class members.

For several reasons the answer to the problem was not revealed to the students during the class. It is valuable for students to have the experience of not knowing for sure and having to rely on their own judgment. There is no doubt that they will need to do this many times in life. Life has no answer book for many situations: Is this the best car to buy? Should I get a mortgage with a fixed or a variable interest rate? Is this a good job to take? Where should I invest my savings? Should I marry this person? Students in school can benefit from the experience of not knowing for sure; while they are still in the safe environment of classrooms we can prepare them for dealing with future uncertainties.

Another reason for not giving the answer is that so long as there is a lack of resolution about the correct answer, the students are more highly motivated to stay involved in thinking about the problem. Revealing an answer too often stops students' thinking about a problem.

At the end of the lesson, students described their solutions and the explanations for their solutions in writing. Because the process of writing helps students clarify their thinking, it is a valuable experience for the students. Also, students' writing provides the teacher with information that is useful for assessing their understandings.

PRESENTING THE PROBLEM

After organizing the students into groups of four, I wrote the problem on the board:

The Horse Problem

A man bought a horse for $50.
He sold it for $60.
Then he bought the horse for $70.
He sold it again for $80.

What is the financial outcome of these transactions? (Ignore cost of feed for the horse, cost of boarding, etc.)

I asked the students to consider in their groups what might be possible solutions to this problem. Their group discussions got animated very quickly, with an audible burst of arguments.

After a few minutes, I interrupted the students and asked for the answers they had thought of. "I'd like to list all of your possible solutions on the board," I said. "I don't want to hear your reasoning just yet, though from listening I can hear that many of you have some strong opinions. Let's hear just the different possible answers."

I listed the six different answers they reported. This list was comparable to what students have offered when I've done the same lesson with other classes:

earned $10
earned $20
lost $10
came out even
earned $40
lost $30

At this time several of the students were so anxious to explain their thinking that they could barely remain in their seats. I told them that we would hear explanations in just a bit, but I wanted first to tell them how we were going to proceed.

"I'm going to designate different places in the room for each of the answers suggested," I told the class. "Once I've established these places, you'll go to the area for the answer you think is best. Then we'll hear reasons for your answers from each of the groups."

I continued with further explanations. "If you haven't decided what you think the answer is, you will be able to stay up here in front until you decide to join a group. Also, it is possible that even though you have a thought now that you'll change your mind after hearing someone else's explanation. That's no problem. All you have to do is walk over and join that group."

Before assigning locations, I asked, "Do you think that after discussion we'll all come to have the same opinion about this problem and wind up standing in the same place?"

Some students weren't sure. Some were sure we would. Others were sure we wouldn't. What was most important to me was that they all seemed interested.

"Let me tell you where all the groups will be before any of you move," I said. "The 'earned $10' group will cluster near Seth's desk. The 'earned $20' group will stand near Amy's desk." I continued designating areas by locating groups near desks where different students were seated, writing the students' names next to the answers so the class could refer back to the list to see where different groups were. When I had designated the location for each of the answers they had identified, I asked them to form their groups.

DISCUSSING THE POSSIBLE SOLUTIONS

When the students had moved to their groups and I had regained their attention, I gave them the next directions. "I will call on a person from each group to explain how you arrived at the answer you chose. I don't want you to formulate a group explanation. I'm interested in hearing individuals' thoughts. That way we may hear more than one explanation for a particular answer."

Karine explains the "earned $10" answer.

I reminded them that they were allowed to change groups. "If an explanation convinces you of an answer, and you are in a different group, feel free to change groups when you change your mind."

Most of the students opted for the "earned $10" and "earned $20" answers, in almost equally sized groups. One boy sat in the "came out even" area. Two boys formed a "lost $30" group. Four undecided students hovered near the front of the room, needing more time or more information before deciding.

My usual tactic at this time is to give the students in the group with the least number of students the chance to offer their arguments first. That gives the minority opinion an initial voice. So I asked Nelson to explain why he thought "came out even" was the best answer.

Nelson is a thoughtful student, competent in his mathematical understanding, confident enough to form a group of one and not run for cover in one of the larger groups. He seemed surprised that he was the only student there, but was willing to explain his reasoning. However, halfway through his explanation he came to a new realization. He stopped in midsentence, grinned at the class, and went to join the "earned $10" group.

I went to the "lost $30" group next. Brian offered his explanation. "The man bought the horse for $50, so he was out $50. Then he sold it for $60, which gave him a $10 profit, so now he was only out $40. He bought it again for $70, so now he is out $110, and sold it for $80. But he was still out $30. He lost $30." The other student in Brian's group nodded in agreement. No one changed groups.

I turned to the "earned $10" group and called on Karine. She explained, "The man bought the horse for $50 and sold it for $60, so he made a $10 profit. But then he bought it again for $70, so that used up his $10 profit, and he was even. Then he sold it for $80 and made another $10. He wound up with $10."

Mark, one of the formerly uncommitted students, went and joined the "earned $10" group. "That's what I was thinking," he said.

Amanda then explained her reason for the "earned $20" answer. "The man bought the horse twice, right? The first time he paid $50, and the second time he paid $70, so he spent $120 on the horse altogether. He sold the horse twice, once for $60 and once for $80. So he sold it altogether for $140. So $140 minus $120 is $20, and that's the profit he made."

Nelson, the boy who had initially been in the "came out even" group, now changed his mind again and joined the "earned $20" group. So did Kathy and Melissa, who had been with the "earned $10" group first.

I turned again to the "lost $30" group, but those students were feeling unsure and opted to pass.

David M. spoke for the "earned $10" group, giving an impassioned plea for his reasoning. Essentially his argument was a restatement of what Karine had offered earlier and was forceful enough to have Kathy and Melissa return. Also at this time two of the uncommitted students went to join the "earned $20" group, leaving only Jerry undecided.

Doug spoke next for the "earned $20" position. "If I started with $100," he said, "and bought a horse for $50, I would have $50. Then if I sold the horse for $60, I would have $110. Then if I bought the horse for $70 I would have $40. If I sold it again for $80 I'd have $120, $20 more than I started out with. That means I earned a $20 profit."

Kathy and Melissa returned to the "earned $20" group. So did Scott, leaving Brian alone in the "lost $30" group. Jerry joined Brian, and the two of them got involved in discussion, going to the chalkboard to work out their figures. Lisl and Jason left the "earned $10" group for the "earned $20" group. The children's regular teacher, to get out of the traffic, sat in an unoccupied desk. The students gaped, wondering why she was sitting in the "came out even" location. "Call on Mrs. Schaefer," Jon called out excitedly. This brought everyone to attention, and we regrouped.

The excitement among the students was very high, and to try to bring a sense of calm to the class, I talked with them a bit. I told them a story, a true story that had happened to me.

"When I was on an airplane once," I said, "I was chatting with the man seated next to me. He was a research physicist who worked for a large company and who was responsible for helping the research scientists communicate with the nonscientists who worked in the company. I told him that I was a teacher, concerned with helping students learn to think mathematically. I told him about the horse problem to illustrate the kind of thinking activities I try to provide for students.

"He said that he had heard the problem before, in a one-day seminar for a group of scientists and nonscientists who were learning how to communicate more effectively with each other. 'The purpose of the problem,' he said, 'was to have us listen to others' points of view and to see how willing we were to change our opinions in the face of new information. The deal was,' he continued, 'that we wouldn't be able to go to lunch until we all agreed.'"

The children had listened to this story attentively. "What happened in his meeting?" Marcie asked.

"He didn't tell me that," I answered. "What he did tell me is that he learned something about himself, which was that it was hard for him to give up his own idea and listen to others."

I continued, relating this to them. "It is hard to listen to other points of view when you have an investment in a different position. Up to now I've heard you offer your own opinions, but not respond to others' ideas. In order to convince others who do not agree with you, I think you need to explain why you think their reasoning isn't correct. Is anyone willing to do that?"

They were still for a bit. Finally, Amy from the "earned $20" group raised her hand. "I have another way to explain the $20 profit that may help," she said. "They are two different business transactions. On each transaction he earns $10, and $10 and $10 make $20 earned altogether."

Karine raised her hand from the "earned $10" group. Before I gave her the opportunity to speak, I asked, "Can you speak to the other arguments offered, Karine?"

She nodded yes and began, "I think the answer you get depends on how you look at it. I can see how you get $20 from what Doug and Amanda and Amy said, but I can also see how you can get $10 from how I see it." And she explained her line of reasoning again.

Several hands shot up in response, most from the "earned $20" group, one from David M., who was still very excited about defending the "earned $10" answer. Rather than recognize any more students, I asked the class a question. "Do you think it is possible that there can be different answers to this problem?" A bellow of no's came from most of the students in the "earned $20" group. A chorus of yes's came from some of the others. In class recently we had been working on problems for which there is more than one answer that is reasonable—tips in a restaurant, how much wood to buy for a project, for example—and some students seemed to be relating the horse problem to that possibility.

I had them disband their groups and take their seats.

ACTING OUT THE PROBLEM

"What is the answer?" Tracy asked once the class was settled.

"As a teacher," I told the class, "I think it is my responsibility to help you understand and solve problems. I'm not convinced that merely telling you the answer will help you understand why that answer is right. I could explain it to you, but you've been doing that for each other, and it doesn't seem to have been convincing for all of you. Rather than tell you the answer or give you my explanation, I'd like to give you another way to think about the problem.

"Here is what I'd like to do," I continued. "I'd like to have the problem acted out; then we'll see if that helps you in thinking about it. What do we need in order to act this out?"

"Money," Marcie said.

There were cards from a fraction game on the table. "We'll use these for money. Each card will be a ten-dollar bill," I told them.

"We need a horse," Scott said, and the class burst out laughing.

"I'll be the horse," Seth volunteered. He came to the front of the room, dropped on all fours, and whinnied.

"What else do we need?" I asked.

"A man to buy the horse," Amy said.

Most students raised their hands, and I chose Jonathan.

"What else?" I asked.

"Another person," several answered, and again most raised their hands. I asked Kathy to take that part.

I then set the stage for the procedure. "Who has the horse to begin with?" I asked.

I received several spontaneous replies. "Jon does." "No, Kathy does." "Yeah, Kathy does."

So I asked Kathy and Seth, the horse, to stand on one side of me and Jonathan on the other. I gave Jonathan $100, having the class count out the "ten-dollar bills" as I gave them to him. I did the same for Kathy.

"After they act out the problem," I said, "what will you want to know?"

There was chorus of answers, so I said, "Please raise your hands so we can hear one response."

I called on Amanda. "We'll want to see how much money Jonathan has to see how much he earned."

"Who will have the horse at the end?" I asked.

There was some confusion with this, but they finally seemed to agree that Kathy would have the horse again.

"Your job," I said to Kathy, Seth, and Jonathan, "is to act out the problem so the rest of the class can clearly see and hear what you are doing." I then addressed the class. "Your job," I said, "is to monitor the action to make sure that what they are doing is consistent with the problem."

I stepped out of the way. The "cast" gave a clear and accurate, but silly, performance, hamming up the problem as much as possible. Especially Seth. When they were done, Jonathan counted out his money. He had $120. A good portion of the class cheered. Others were ready to argue, some feeling that the problem would come out differently if I hadn't given them each $100 at the start.

At this time they were quite excited. I asked the actors to take their seats and got the class quiet.

A TIME FOR INDIVIDUAL REFLECTION

"I'm interested in what you are each thinking," I told the class, "and I want to take the time now for you to explain your thoughts. All this has been exciting and active. Right now I'd like the room quiet. I'd like each of you to sit with your thoughts quietly for a moment before putting them in writing, describing your thinking as completely as possible. When you've finished, please bring your paper to me and then find some quiet reading to do while others continue to work."

The class got very quiet, and slowly students began their writing. As I watched them work on their thoughts, I noticed how much more willing they were to do the writing this time than they had been when I had first asked them to write in math class. I think it was because they now knew that I was interested in their thinking because I believed it was important. Also, they had had practice in expressing their thoughts, and had been finding it easier with each opportunity.

Six of the students wrote explanations of why the answer could be either $10 or $20. One defended $10 as the best answer. Sixteen were convinced that the correct answer was $20. Following is a sampling of their responses.

From Jason: *I think that the answer is the man earns $20 because I said to myself, "Let's say the man gets a loan for $100 at the bank. Then he buy's a horse for $50 so he has $50. Then he sold the horse for $60, so he has $110 but then he buys it back for $70 so he has $40, but then he sold it back for $80 so he has $120, but he has to pay back the loan for $100 and he ends up with $20.*

From Seth: *I think that this problem was difficult. There were a few traps in it and that made it difficult. I still think the answer is earn $10 because it can'be $20 because you gave the first $10 away when you bought it for $70.*

From Kathy: *First I was on the ten side. But then I heard a good statement from the 20 side so I went to the 20 side. Then I heard from the 10 side and I thought that was right so I went back to the 10 side. Then Doug said*

I think that the answer is the man earns $20 because ~~he~~ I said to myself, "Let's say the man gets a loan for $100 at the bank. Then he buys a horse for $50 so he has $50. Then he sold the horse for $60, so he has $110. but then he buys it back for $70 so he has $40, but then he sold it back for $80 so he has $120, but he has to pay back the loan for $100 and he ends up with $20.

Jason Mizrahi

In Jason's explanation, the man begins by getting a bank loan.

something that was very good. It made a lot of sense so I went back and I was right.

From Karine: *I think it could be earn $20 or earn $10. It depends which way you look at the problem. There could be many different answers but my decision is either gain $10 or $20.*

From Kasara: *I think that he made $20.00 as a profit. If you add up what he sold the horse for (the two times he sold the horse) it was $140. Then you add up how much money he used to buy the horse (the two times he bought the horse) I got $120. I subtracted and got 20 dollars. $140 − $120 = $20.00.*

From Scott: *I think it is 20 because of mainly the demonstration in front of the room even though I thought it all along.*

From Amy: *I think the answer to the horse problem is that he earned 20 dollars. There are many different ways of figuring this out.*

One way is to add his earnings and add his spendings and last subtract his spendings from his earnings.

Another way is to say there are two different business transactions. On each transaction he earns 10 dollars. 10 dollars and 10 dollars equals 20 dollars earned.

From Jerry, who had been uncommitted much of the time, an explanation of both possible "prophets": *I think he makes $20 prophet and $10*

Amy gives two explanations for her solution to the horse problem.

prophet. *Let's say he starts with $50. He loses that money by buying the horse. Then he makes a $10 prophet by selling the horse for $60. The person has to borrow $10 to buy the horse again for $70. Then he sells the horse again and makes a 10 prophet which he has to use to pay back his debt. Then he has ten dollars left. So the answer is $10 prophet.*

Let's say the person starts with $100. He buys a horse for $50 and has $50 left. Then he sells the horse for $60 so now he has $110 left. He buys it back for $70 so he has $40 left. Then he sells it back again for $80. Then he ends up with $120 so he makes a $20 prophet.

From Brian, who stayed with his "lost $30" until talking with Jerry: *I think that $20 is right all the way now because I did it with Jerry and in my head and then acted it out.*

I did this problem with the class on their last day of math class for the year. That accounted for some of the level of excitement. We spent a little more than one hour on the activity as described. Though it was a hectic hour, the spirit and thinking that were evident made it a wonderful way to end the year's math learning.

Working with a group helps when looking for all the pentominoes.

I t is important for students in the elementary grades to have hands-on experiences to develop understanding of concepts in geometry. This lesson with sixth graders models such an experience. Students use one-inch-square tiles and paper ruled into one-inch squares to solve the problem of finding all the possible ways to arrange five squares into shapes called pentominoes. This problem-solving activity gives the students a common base of experience for studying several geometric ideas.

The concept of congruence becomes key as students try to find all the different pentominoes. In order to compare the figures they create, students explore geometric transformations, including translations (slides), rotations (turns), and reflections (flips). In a follow-up activity, investigating which of their pentominoes will fold into boxes, students relate their two-dimensional exploration to three-dimensional shapes. Also, the students explore the concepts of perimeter and mirror symmetry as they sort their pentomino shapes.

This lesson is an especially rich geometry experience. It gives students the opportunity to explore several geometry concepts at the same time, which helps students to see the relationship of one concept to another. The exploration helps students develop their perception of spatial relationships. In addition, the activity necessitates students' deciding when they have found all possible pentominoes, thus requiring that they apply logical reasoning to a spatial task.

BEGINNING THE LESSON

This sixth-grade class is one I have taught on a regular basis. The students are accustomed to working in small cooperative groups. Their individual desks are grouped into clusters of four, with groups of three or five as needed to accommodate all the students. The students were told yesterday that I would teach today's math lesson and that it would be a problem-solving activity to launch a unit on geometry.

When I arrived, the thirty-one students were seated in eight groups, seven groups of four and one group of three. I distributed materials to each group—twenty one-inch tiles, enough for each students to have five, and two sheets of dittoed squared paper.

I then began the lesson by telling the class that in this problem-solving activity, they would search for different shapes that could be made from five squares, using the tiles I had distributed. "These shapes made from five squares are called pentominoes," I explained, writing the word *pentominoes* on the chalkboard. "There are three ideas you will need to understand in doing this activity.

"First of all," I continued, "there is a rule you will need to follow when making pentomino shapes. When you arrange the squares into shapes, the requirement is that at least one whole side of each square touches a whole side of another." I drew the following examples on the chalkboard and labeled them:

This is OK: This is not OK:

"Second," I went on, "you will have to decide if the shapes you create are the same or different. That's where the squared paper will come in handy.

Here are two legal shapes." I drew them on the board: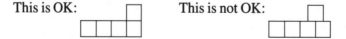

Then I cut each from a sheet of the squared paper and showed how to use the cut-out shapes to compare them.

"I can move these, flipping one and turning it like this so it fits exactly on the other. Even though they look different the way I drew them on the board, they can be moved to match each other exactly. Because of this, they are considered to be the same shape. Does anyone know the word that describes two figures that are exactly the same size and the same shape?"

A few volunteered responses: "Matching." "Equal." "Congruent." "Exact."

"The correct mathematical term is *congruent*," I told them. I explained once again, "If two cut-out shapes fit exactly, they are called congruent and count as only one shape."

Finally, I discussed the derivation of the word *pentomino*. I drew a picture of a domino on the board and could tell from their murmurs that they recognized the shape. I explained, "A domino is made from two squares. The pentominoes you will explore are five-square versions. What do you think a three-square version might be called?"

After several predictions, I wrote the word *tromino* on the board. I also wrote the word *tetromino,* telling them that is what four-square shapes are called.

After this introduction, I posed a problem to the class that is similar to but less complex than the pentomino exploration I would ask them to begin shortly. "Suppose we were trying to find all the different arrangements of three squares, all the different trominoes. What shapes could we make?"

Lisa volunteered immediately, "They could be in a straight row," and I drew that possibility on the board.

Kenny said, "You could make an L," and I drew that also.

"I've got one," Todd said, but when he looked up from his desk and noticed what I had already drawn on the board, he corrected himself, "Oh, no, you've already got that L."

"I've got a different L," Leah offered. But Jennifer, one of her group members, told her that it would look the same if she just turned it upside-down. Leah looked up at the drawing on the board and back at the shape at her desk a few times and finally rotated the shape on her desk to convince herself that the two L's were indeed the same. Merely looking hadn't been enough.

"Cutting them out of paper will give you a way to prove whether two shapes are congruent," I reminded them.

I felt that the class understood what had been presented so far and decided to get them started on their problem. (If I had thought they were at all shaky, I would have had them search for the different tetrominoes, the shapes from four squares.)

I then presented the problem to be solved. "In your groups you are to find all the possible ways to arrange five squares into pentominoes. You are to cut each of them out of the squared paper provided. As a group you should make one set of all the different pentominoes, accounting for all the possible arrangements. Are there any questions?"

"How many shapes are we supposed to find?" Scott asked. I, and the class, have learned to expect Scott to ask that kind of clarifying question.

"That's part of the problem for your group to solve, to find all the pentominoes and to convince yourselves that you have found all the possible arrangements there are. Let me know when you think you've done that and I'll come and discuss what your group has done."

There were no other questions.

DURING THE EXPLORATION

As the students got to work exploring the problem, the noise level rose in the room, but it was the productive kind of noise that was purposeful, not frantic. The class seemed focused and interested in the problem. With this class, as in others, whenever the students have the opportunity to handle materials, they seem to get interested more easily than on abstract, paper-and-pencil problems.

I circulated as they worked. I checked on Leah to make sure she was moving along with the others and decided that she seemed to be doing fine. During this exploring time, I stay out of their group interactions as much as possible. I listen casually to their comments, noticing how individual students are working. I note ideas I overhear that will be useful for later discussion. I am ready to offer assistance when all group members raise their hands, as they've learned to do when they need help, or when I feel a group is totally bogged down.

After almost twenty minutes, a group called me over. "We think we've found them all," they announced.

"How many do you have?" I asked.

They did a quick count of their cut-out shapes. "Nine. No, ten."

As I scanned their shapes, a nearby group that had overheard them chimed in, "We have eleven." I told the second group that I'd be there in a moment and refocused on the first group. I noticed that two of their shapes were congruent. "Examine your shapes again," I told them. "I see two that are really the same. See if you can find those, and then see if you can discover any new ones."

The group seemed a little discouraged, but Mark got them back on track. "I see them," he said, picking up the two congruent shapes. Mark is usually motivated to continue a search and can be counted on to keep a group probing. It didn't surprise me that the group with Mark in it was the first to call me over.

I moved to the second group. "We found another," they told me. "Now we have twelve, and we think we have them all." I looked over their shapes and noticed in their arrangements also that two were the same. "I see two that are congruent," I told them, moving away. I heard Susie comment, "Let's find those and then look some more. There can't be just eleven. There are never eleven of anything."

Another group signaled for me by raising their hands. It's often at this stage in a problem-solving activity that the class gets a bit hectic. This group had found eight shapes and seemed satisfied. "The group with Mark in it has found nine, and the group with Susie has found eleven," I told them. "Keep looking." They groaned a bit, but got back to work.

One more group was ready. They had found twelve, all different, and felt calmly secure and satisfied. "We think we found them all," they announced.

"Tell me why you think that," I responded.

Scott explained. "We know there is only one with all five in a row. Then we looked for shapes with four in a row. Then with three. There were lots of those. Then two. We threw out the doubles." This explanation is typically Scott. He usually provides the leadership in thinking.

"Do we have them all?" Sara asked, not having Scott's confidence and needing to know.

"Yes," I answered them, "but don't announce this to the others. Let's give them some more time to search. In the meantime here's a puzzle you can work on using your pieces. See if you can get all twelve of your pieces to fit together into one large rectangle. How many squares are there in all with your twelve pieces?"

They thought a bit. Kenny jotted down 12 x 5 on a piece of scrap paper and came up with 60. "So," I continued, "a large rectangle will use all sixty squares. What dimensions might it have?"

"Ten by six," Sara answered quickly. "Will that work?" she asked, again needing to know.

"I'm not sure," I responded honestly, "but I've fit them into a five-by-twelve rectangle and into a three by twenty. I don't know how many different ways there are to do it. Maybe you can find out."

By this time two other groups had their hands raised. One was the group with Susie in it. "We have twelve now," they said. I directed them to ask the group with Scott and Sara in it to explain the puzzle activity to them. When I approached the other group, they waved me away, having gotten back to work. They had probably heard Susie's group report that they had found twelve and were willing to look some more.

One more group raised their hands to announce that they were done. They had ten shapes, all different. "I've seen two other groups with those same ten shapes, and more," I told them. "See if you can find others."

SUMMARIZING THE ACTIVITY

After another few minutes, I decided to interrupt the entire class for a discussion. It took a while to get their attention and to settle them down.

"Let's summarize this activity," I said when I had their attention. "Let's talk first about how you got organized as a group. I'd like you to hear from each other."

Mark posts his group's pentominoes for the class.

Sara started. "Scott organized us. He wanted us to look for shapes in a system. We did it his way."

"Did you understand his system?" I asked.

"Not really at first," Sara answered, "but then as we got into it, I kind of caught on. I was able to find some shapes, though."

"How about another group?" I asked.

Jennifer responded. "We just all started working, and when someone found a shape, they told the rest, and we looked to see if it was a new one or not. Then they cut it out."

"We did it the same way," Mike offered, "but Stephanie did all the cutting out."

"Why did you decide to do that?" I asked.

Stephanie answered. "We really didn't decide. I just did it." The class giggled.

"Did it work well for you?" I pursued.

The group looked at each other and nodded. "I think so," Mike said. "I liked it," Stephanie said. Stephanie likes being organized and often offers to do the kinds of chores that keep things orderly.

"Are there any other ways groups organized that were different?" I continued. I waited a bit. None was offered. "What about the problem of finding the pentominoes? Was it hard, easy, enjoyable, unpleasant? How did you feel about searching for all the shapes? Do you think your group solved the problem?" No comments were immediately offered. I waited, having learned that the students need the time to think that a few moments of silence can provide.

Finally Jennifer raised her hand. "It started off being easy, but then it got hard to find more." Some murmurs of assent went through the class.

"What did you do when it got hard?" I asked.

Jennifer responded, "Oh, we just kept looking. I found that when I just kept moving the tiles around, I would find a new shape. Then we had to check all the ones we had."

Steve agreed. "It was real hard once we got ten. We knew there were more because you had said that Mark's group had eleven."

"What did you do then?" I asked.

"We went and looked at his group's shapes," Steve confessed. Giggles again from the class.

"How did you tell which ones you didn't have?" I asked.

"That wasn't easy," Steve said. "It was hard to figure that out. We had to bring our pieces over."

"Where was I when all this was going on?" I asked, wondering how I had missed it. The class laughed.

Kirsten, also in Steve's group, offered an explanation. "Oh, you were talking to Scott's group. You were real busy."

"Are there really twelve shapes?" Leah asked.

"Yes," I replied. "How about one group that has found them all posting theirs so the other groups can see which ones they're missing. I want each group to have a complete set for tomorrow's activity. Also, I will give each of you a piece of centimeter squared paper on which you should sketch all twelve shapes for an individual record. You'll need that for tomorrow as well. There are lots of other geometry ideas I want you to investigate using your pentomino pieces. Who will post the pieces?"

Mark volunteered to do so, and I gave him a box of pins so he could pin the pentominoes in a corner of the bulletin board. I put out a stack of centimeter paper for the students to use to make their individual recordings and suggested that one person from each group come get enough for the entire group. I had Stephanie pass out a small envelope to each group for the pentomino pieces. "Take some time now to make your own recordings and to clean up the scraps of paper," I instructed. "Label the envelope for your pentomino pieces with your group name. I'll keep the envelopes for tomorrow. If you have time and are interested in a puzzle, check with Kenny's group to learn one you can do with your pentomino pieces."

The class got busy again, finishing up, organizing. I felt good about this lesson. The students were working well together and were approaching these kinds of problem situations more eagerly than they had when the year began. That they were able to suspend their need for the answer of how many pentominoes there were was a sign, I believed, that good attitudes toward solving problems were being developed in the class.

EXTENDING THE EXPERIENCE

As the students were finishing up, I discussed with the children's teacher how I would like to structure additional lessons. I wanted the groups to sort their shapes into two sets, those that would and those that would not fold into boxes. That way the students would experience relating two-dimensional shapes to a three-dimensional one, a cube with one face missing.

I planned to introduce this activity by starting with the shape that looks like the Red Cross symbol: . I would ask the students to visualize how they could fold up the sides of this shape so that it would be a box without a lid. Students then would predict which side they thought would be the bottom of the box, opposite the open side, and would mark their prediction with an X on the appropriate square on their group's pentomino. Then I would model for them how to fold the pentomino shape to check their prediction.

For each of the other pentominoes, students would individually inspect the pentominoes on their individual record sheets to predict whether or not each would fold into a box. They then would compare predictions with their group members. They would discuss which squares should be marked with an X to indicate the bottom of the boxes. Finally, they would test their predictions, using their group set of cut-out pentomino shapes. Some students are very weak on these types of activities, and this sort of experience can help them strengthen those skills and build their confidence in doing so.

I had other follow-up experiences for the pentomino pieces that I planned to have the class try. The groups could sort the shapes in several ways. Students could fold each of the pieces to decide which have mirror symmetry and which do not and also find which have more than one line of symmetry. They could also sort them by their perimeters, providing a concrete experience with the notion that shapes with the same area do not necessarily have the same perimeter.

As another follow-up, each student makes a set of pentomino pieces from sturdy paper. Everyone also makes a five-by-twelve squared sheet as a gameboard, with squares matching the size of the squares used for the pentominoes. As an individual puzzle, each student uses the board and pieces, trying to fit all twelve pieces onto the board, the puzzle some groups had already begun to explore. As a two-person game, players take turns placing pieces on the board, with the object being to play the last possible piece so that it is impossible for the opponent to fit in another. These games could go home as family gifts to help students communicate what sorts of things they were doing in their math class.

School milk cartons are useful for a further follow-up activity, for which students need to save enough school milk cartons so each student can have several. The cartons should be rinsed well, and the tops must be cut off, making them topless boxes. For this exploration students try cutting the milk cartons so they will lie flat in the different pentomino shapes they have chosen.

As long as the interest holds, pentomino pieces can be used to provide experiences with different geometric concepts. This kind of investigation, which extends over time, is valuable for giving students time to digest and process what they are learning.

"How many times will I have to draw a cube to get one of each of the six colors?"

I nstruction in mathematics should provide students with experiences in which concepts and skills from the different strands of the math curriculum are interwoven. Too often children study the different topics of mathematics separately. They learn skills and concepts in isolation and do not necessarily learn to see the relationship of one concept to another.

Presenting mathematics concepts in isolation is similar to presenting all the pieces of a puzzle and giving no clue as to how the pieces fit together. Too many children never succeed in making the connections for themselves and therefore never develop an adequate understanding or appreciation for math.

This lesson with six graders models an experience for students in which they use concepts and skills from different mathematical topics to investigate a situation. A range of mathematical concepts is used in this particular lesson. In the area of number, students are asked to focus on ratio and proportion and fractional equivalence.

In the area of statistics, students collect, organize, represent, and interpret data, are introduced to a frequency distribution, and explore mean, median, mode, and range. In the area of probability, students discuss the representation of the probability of an event. All of these concepts are appropriate content for six graders.

A teacher may choose to present this lesson to students because it addresses a specific concept the class is studying—averages, for example. However, the benefit of a lesson such as this one is its broad scope. More than dealing with one specific concept, it illustrates the connections among concepts.

The lesson described fits the content of the mathematics curriculum and has benefit for students at other grade levels as well. Third graders, for example, may not bring understanding about fractional equivalence or averages to the activity; however, they will certainly benefit from collecting, organizing, representing, and interpreting the data that emerge from the experiments. The lesson can also be of benefit to high school students as a way to use more sophisticated mathematical procedures to make predictions about the possible outcomes of the experiments. As with the best of the classic children's books that hold appeal for readers of all ages, an effective mathematical experience is one that holds wonder and intrigue for learners of all ages.

PRESENTING THE SITUATION

The situation I described to the class was adapted from the Perky Popcorn activity created by the Equals group at the Lawrence Hall of Science in Berkeley, California. The students were seated randomly in groups of four, and I began by describing the problem to the class.

"A popcorn company found that sales improved when special treats and surprises were included in the boxes of popcorn," I told the class. "This particular company has recently put a picture card in each box of popcorn. The pictures are of famous mathematicians, and there are six mathematicians in the complete set."

I paused and then pointed out, "Everyone can hardly wait to collect a complete set."

"Is this really true?" John asked, with a skeptical look on his face.

"No, it's not a real company. It's a made-up problem, but it presents a situation similar to one that does exist for some companies," I explained to the class.

"Like collecting cards from bubble gum," Tim added.

I nodded and continued with my story. "The owners of the popcorn company try to make collecting a complete set as fair as possible. Not only have they printed an equal number of each of the six different cards, but also when they ship the popcorn to stores, they are very careful to ship the same number of each mathematician. When you buy a box, you have an equal chance of getting any one of the six different cards."

I then posed a problem for them to consider, "About how many boxes of popcorn do you think you would have to buy in order to get a complete set of six mathematicians?"

Several hands quickly went up from students willing to respond. However, I waited, allowing time for others as well to give the question some thought. Then, rather than having individual students offer their thoughts to the entire class, I asked them to discuss their predictions with each other in their small groups. The use of small groups creates the opportunity for more students to share their thoughts than is possible in a class discussion.

After their group discussions, I called for responses. They were varied. They included specific predictions: "12." "100." "18." "14." "36." Also possible ranges: "Between 15 and 20." "Somewhere from 20 to 40." "Anywhere from 6 to 1,000."

Some students reported speculative guesses without being able to justify them. Others had reasons. Sara offered hers, "18, because that gives you three chances to get each one, and that sounds possible." Robert explained, "36 because 6 times 6 is 36." John, always literal and skeptical, claimed, "Anywhere from 6 to 1,000 because you really can't tell." Manda said, "I think it would take about 15 boxes because it would take a while to get 6 cards because you'd get doubles."

I then gave the students time to describe their predictions in writing. I wrote the question for them to consider on the board: About how many boxes of popcorn do you think you'd have to buy to get a complete set of six mathematicians? Explain your reasoning. I told them that it was OK if they chose to change their minds from what they had initially reported, that I was interested in what they now were thinking.

Andrea wrote: *It would take between 10 and 18 boxes because the first box would give you one mathematician so you need about two tries for each of the other cards.*

David wrote: *I think you need 36 boxes of popcorn to get the set. That way you get 6 chances for all six cards.*

From Russell: *6, 12, or forever.*

From Lori: *I think it would take between 15 and 25 boxes because it is all luck, but since there are only 6 cards, how unlucky can someone be?*

Jill wrote: *I think between 12-15 boxes of popcorn because it's rare to get all six mathematicians in six boxes, because that's luck. I think that you will get doubles and it'll take you at least 12-15 boxes of popcorn to get all six mathematicians.*

And from Jeff: *I think 20 because you can get the same cards again.*

I then told the class, "The difficulty in such a situation is that we really can't find out. We don't have access to all these popcorn boxes since the problem is not a real one. And even if we did, the best way to solve the

I think 20 because you can get the same cards again.

I think you need 36 boxes of popcorn. to get the set. That way you get 6 chances for all six cards.

It could be any amount because you might get two or three of the same card.

I think it's not easy to tell because you can't know what's in the box before you open it.

I think 12 boxes of popcorn because if you bought 6 theres more of a chance of not getting all six It would be luck. I think theres a better chance with 12.

Students offer a variety of initial predictions and explanations.

problem might not be to munch our way through box after box of popcorn. In real life we often face problems that can't be solved directly, where we have to make predictions when we do not have access to all the information we would like.

"In such cases," I continued, "one thing that is possible is to devise an

Variety in the recordings results when students are given responsibility for organizing their data.

experiment that will give us information about the situation we face. Such an experiment is called a simulation, and it is something that mathematicians do often in order to make decisions.

"We are going to do a simulation here in class," I told them, "that will give us information to help us decide about the popcorn problem. So for now we'll put the popcorn on the shelf and turn our attention to an experiment."

STRUCTURING THE SIMULATION ACTIVITY

I took a paper lunch sack and put six cubes into it, one each of six different colors. "In relation to the popcorn problem, why do you think I put cubes of six colors in the sack?" I asked the class.

"Because of the six mathematicians," several students responded simultaneously.

I reached into the sack without looking, drew out one cube, and held it up for the class to see. "Note that the cube is red," I said to the students. I replaced the cube, shook the sack, and repeated the procedure. I drew another cube, asked the students to note its color, replaced it, and shook the sack again.

I then asked the class to make a prediction, "How many times will I have to repeat this procedure before I have drawn one of each of the six colors?"

Following the convention I used before, I gave them time to think individually first, then asked them to discuss their thoughts with their groups,

Students try the experiment in their groups.

and finally had them report to the class. Their conclusions were similar to the predictions they had made for the popcorn problem. The students seemed willing to accept that this experiment with the cubes would help them with the popcorn situation, and they were anxious to get started.

I outlined the task for them, "Each group will have a sack with six different-colored cubes and one sheet of paper on which to record your group work. First your group needs to decide how you will organize the experiment and record your results. Then you are to do the experiment as many times as you can before I ask you to stop. After that, groups will report their results, including how you recorded your work, and we'll discuss the experiment as a class."

The groups got enthusiastically busy. This was no surprise. After all, here was an opportunity for them to be actively involved in an investigation, working with the support of the other students in small groups, searching to understand a situation. This was a contrast to their more traditional mathematics experiences of working individually to find correct and exact solutions.

Also, using the cubes for this experiment was appealing to the students. Besides their appeal, however, concrete materials provide a way for stu-

How many draws?

6		17	
7		18	I
8	IIII	19	
9	II	20	
10	II	21	
11	I	22	
12	II	23	I
13	I	24	
14	III	25	
15	I	26	
16	I	27	

A frequency distribution organizes the students' results.

dents to connect the understandings that can be gleaned from relating real objects to mathematical concepts.

After circulating to see that they were all tackling the experiment correctly, I prepared a chart on the chalkboard, listing the numbers from 6 to 27. I began the list with 6 because it represented the fewest draws possible, and I stopped at 27 because I had filled up two columns on the chalkboard. I could add more numbers if they were needed.

When I interrupted the students, each of the eight groups in the class had completed the experiment at least twice. I had a student from each group report how they had recorded their work. Each student came to the front of the room for the presentation and showed the group's record sheets. From this, students saw different models for collecting, organizing, and representing data.

I then had them report their results, and I marked each on my chart with a tally, making a frequency chart of the class results. They had done the experiment nineteen times in all. I focused the class on the chart in several ways.

I told them that this record was a frequency distribution, and I explained why I had started my list with the number 6. This seemed obvious to them. I then asked, "What was the fewest number of draws it took to get one of each of the six colors?" Several quickly answered that 8 was the fewest number of draws. "What was the most number of draws it took?" I asked. They read 23 from the chart. I then explained what is meant by the range in such a distribution, illustrating this idea with the specifics from the class data.

I then discussed the ideas of mean, median, and mode with them. No instruction on these concepts had been done yet this year, and this activity seemed to provide an appropriate reason for introducing them. I wanted the students to get some understanding of these three different ways of looking at the idea of average. Having students learn concepts in the contexts where they occur makes good sense for math instruction.

I brought the students' attention to the number of draws that had occurred most often, which was 8, and told them this was called the mode. Then I listed all the results in order, having them help by reading the information from the chart. Four 8s were followed by two 9s, one 10, one 11, two 12's, and so on down to the one 23. We found the middle one in the list, one of the 12s, and I told them this was the median. Then we calculated the mean, and I modeled adding the numbers mentally for them. The mean came out to be just a bit more than 12. "It would be much easier to do this with a calculator," I told them, "but since I didn't have mine handy, I figured it out."

I then focused on probability and asked the students if they knew the probability of drawing a cube of a specific color, a red cube, for example, when reaching into the sack. Several responded that it was one out of six, and I explained that the fraction $1/6$ is used to represent this probability.

It was now the end of the period, and I told the students we would return to this investigation the next day.

EXTENDING THE SIMULATION

When math class began the next day, I told the class that I would like to return to the popcorn problem by trying an additional experiment. "This experiment," I explained, "is similar to the one you did yesterday. However, instead of having one each of six different colors in the sack, you will have ten each of the six colors, a total of sixty cubes in the sack."

"What do you think will be the results from this experiment?" I asked. "Do you think it will take more draws, fewer draws, or about the same number of draws before one of each color has been drawn from the sack?" I was curious to see if they would be able to connect concepts about ratio and proportion to a probability situation.

I allowed all who volunteered to share their thoughts. Students' opinions differed. Many felt that it would take more draws, and their reasons were variations on the theme that because there were so many cubes, it would be harder to get one of each. Some felt that it should be the same as the first experiment.

Having students explain their thinking is extremely important to their learning. By explaining their ideas in their own words, students have the opportunity to explore, clarify, and cement their understanding of math concepts. A testimony to this emerged from Russell's explanation, "I think that it will take more draws because if you needed just 1 more color, like yellow, you would have to be lucky to pick a yellow out of all 60 cubes, instead of just having to pick it out of 6 cubes . . . but wait a minute . . . there are more yellows in the sack, so you have 10 chances instead of 1 chance to pick out a yellow cube, and 10 out of 60 is the same as

1 out of 6, so it should take the same." Russell sat back, convinced and sure in his conclusion. Though a few other students agreed, most were not convinced.

I probed further, encouraging students to share their thinking. "How do you know that 10 out of 60 is the same as 1 out of 6?" "Can anyone explain that another way?" "Does anyone have a different thought?" It is from listening to students' explanations that I can get insights into students' understanding, so that I can decide in which direction further instruction needs to go. Also, hearing others' ideas helps students gain perspective on their own thinking.

The groups then tried the experiment using sixty cubes in each sack. I created another chart on the chalkboard, next to the one we had used yesterday. This time I had the students record their results as they completed their experiments. They did twenty-one experiments in all. Again we figured the mode, median, and mean. From this set of statistics, the range was from 6 to 24. The mode was again 8, the median was 9, and the mean was almost 12.

Most of the students were quite surprised at the similarity in the information from the two distributions. It was evident that most were not able to use the ideas of ratio and proportion to explain the results.

SUMMARIZING THE LESSON

The summarizing of any lesson is essential for its mathematical potential to be nurtured. This is a time when students are encouraged to consider what they have experienced in relation to the mathematics involved, to see connections between this and other experiences, to reflect on their thinking. I raised a variety of questions.

1. How can you explain the relationship between the experiments with the cubes and the popcorn problem?
2. How can you justify the validity of the decisions you reached about the popcorn situation from the results of these experiments?
3. What results from the experiments would you expect if the numbers of cubes differed, if there were three, or four, or ten colors, for example, instead of six?
4. Instead of experiments using cubes to simulate the popcorn problem, suppose you used a die, seeing how many times it needed to be tossed before each of the numbers from 1 to 6 come up? Why would or why wouldn't this be a sensible simulation?
5. What do you think you have learned from this lesson?

The students' responses to these questions gave me information that I could use to plan further activities that would be both of value and interest to them.

To end the class I had the students again write individually to explain how many boxes of popcorn they now thought they would have to buy in

Melissa explains her thinking at the end of the lesson.

order to get a complete set of six mathematicians. I structured the assignment by telling them to title their paper After Doing the Experiments with the Cubes. I told them to begin by writing "Now I think . . ."

John wrote: *Now I think it would take about 12 boxes because you have to buy that much because a couple of times you get the same cards over again.*

Tim was impressed with the mode: *Now I think I'd have to buy 8 boxes of popcorn because that is what people got most on the experiment.*

David changed his mind from his orginal prediction of 36: *Now I think I'd need to buy 8-12 bags of popcorn because that was the range of averages for both experiments.*

Melissa wrote: *Now I think I'd have to buy 12 bags of popcorn because you can get six different cubes in six different try's, but I think that is just luck. I think your bound to get doubles of something because when we did the experiment we got at least 3 doubles. That's why I think it's twelve.*

Sara relied heavily on the statistical results: *Now I think I'd have to buy 12 boxes of popcorn because on both charts the average was 12 and I think that because it was 12 both times it makes sense to me that it would be 12. Also the chances of you getting a different color is the same amount in each kind of bag. So since the mean was 12 on both charts, I will stick with 12.*

···0-99 CHART···

☐ 1-step
■ 2-step
▨ 3-step
▦ 4-step

Lisa is pleased with the symmetry in the 0-99 chart pattern.

Numbers that are palindromes read the same frontward and backward, such as 88, 252, and 4,004. (What is the next year that is a palindrome?) A relationship between numbers that are palindromes and are not palindromes has long been known by mathematicians. If a number is not palindromic, it can be converted to a palindrome by a special procedure — reverse its digits and add the two numbers. With 16, for example, reversing its digits produces 61; 16 plus 61 is 77 — a palindrome. If the sum produced is not a palindrome, then the procedure must be repeated, reversing its digits and adding until the sum appears as a palindrome.

There is a conjecture concerning palindromes that this "reverse and add" procedure will always lead to a palindrome. As yet, however, the conjecture has never been proved. Also, it has been reported that the number 196, even after 4,147 reversals, fails to generate a palindrome. (Perhaps some future computer investigation will go even further.)

Palindromes   159

However, for numbers smaller than 100, all convert to palindromes. And all except for 98 and 89 take six or fewer reversals to do so. This lesson presents to a class of sixth graders the mathematical investigation of converting the numbers from 0 to 99 to palindromes.

Exploring palindromes is a valuable classroom experience for a variety of reasons. Because the investigation requires only the arithmetic skill of addition, it is an activity suitable for students of varying ability levels. Also, the arithmetic practice provided by the activity provokes much more interest than do standard drill exercises, a situation which contributes to helping students see mathematics as interesting and enjoyable. Another benefit of the exploration is that students are challenged to use several higher-order thinking skills — they look for and analyze patterns, they make conjectures and test their validity, and they formulate generalizations.

Along with these educational benefits, investigating palindromes is an activity that seems to have great appeal to students. The sixth graders described in this lesson worked diligently over a period of a week — adding, searching for patterns, comparing discoveries. Their perseverance was the indicator that the activity was both intriguing and satisfying for them.

The class was accustomed to working in small cooperative groups and sat in groups of four regularly. This activity, however, is a good beginning one for classes that have not had much experience working cooperatively because students immediately perceive the benefit of having a group to share both the labor and the thinking.

EXPLAINING PALINDROMES

In preparation for this lesson, I duplicated two worksheets for each of the students. I distributed them to the students and began my introduction.

"Palindromes are numbers that read the same frontward and backward," I told the class. I then gave them some examples, "44 is a palindrome. So are 252 and 8,008." I wrote those numbers on the board as I mentioned them and then asked, "What is the next year that will be a palindrome?"

Several hands went up. I called on Mark. "2002," he said.

"That's not it," Kirsten called out.

"Isn't 2002 a palindrome?" I asked Kirsten.

"It's a palindrome," she answered, "but there's a year that comes sooner — 1991." The class agreed.

Lisa raised her hand, and I called on her. "My house number is one. It's 44."

"I have a question," I said next. "Do you think there are more numbers that are palindromes or numbers that are not palindromes? Discuss this for a bit in your groups; then I'll have you share your thoughts with each other."

The class was accustomed to discussing in their groups, and heads immediately went together. I prefer to have the class talk in small groups before having a discussion with the entire class. I think that more of the students get the chance to express their ideas in groups than if I call on just a few to respond to the entire class.

After a few minutes, I interrupted the groups for a class discussion. I reminded them that they needed to explain their reasoning for their answers as we had done in previous experiences. I called on Scott first.

"There have to be more numbers that aren't palindromes," he said, "because if you just look at the numbers from 1 to 100, there are only nine — 11, 22, 33, 44, 55, 66, 77, 88, and 99."

Stephanie's hand shot up, and I called on her. "We also think there are more numbers that aren't palindromes," she said, "but we think that 1, 2, 3, 4, 5, 6, 7, 8, and 9 are palindromes too."

"Which is it?" Leah asked. "Do they count?" She wanted a judgment as to whether single-digit numbers are palindromes.

"That question will be easier to answer after I introduce you to the activity with palindromes I'd like you to try," I answered. I don't like giving I'll-tell-you-later responses, but in this case I felt that the question would be better answered when they had some more information.

I refocused them on the question I had raised. "Is there a different opinion about whether there are more palindromes or nonpalindromes?" I asked. "Or are there any other reasons to support your opinion?"

Steve raised his hand. "In any hundred numbers, there aren't very many palindromes," he said, then explained further. "In the 100s, the last number has to be a 1, and then there are only ten numbers you can make. Here, I'll show you." Steve came to the board and listed ten numbers — 101, 111, 121, 131, 141, 151, 161, 171, 181, and 191. He then said, "It's the same for the 200s and the 300s and so on, so there aren't too many palindromes."

This seemed to close the issue for the class.

I continued with my introduction. "Mathematicians have found that a number that is not a palindrome can be changed into a palindrome by adding in a certain way. Take 13, for instance." I wrote 13 on the chalkboard and continued, "You reverse the digits and add." I wrote 31 under the 13 and added:

$$\begin{array}{r} 13 \\ +31 \\ \hline 44 \end{array}$$

"Not all numbers are so cooperative," I continued, "and you have to continue to reverse and add before it works. I'll show you with 68." I did the process on the board, explaining as I did it:

$$\begin{array}{r} 68 \\ +\ 86 \\ \hline 154 \\ +\ 451 \\ \hline 605 \\ +\ 506 \\ \hline 1111 \end{array}$$

"How many additions did it take me to change 13 into a palindrome?" I asked. In response to their answer of one, I circled the one addition sign and said, "Changing 13 into a palindrome takes a one-step operation."

"How many additions did 68 take?" I asked. They answered correctly, and I circled the addition signs and said, "So 68 requires a three-step operation."

In order to make sure they understood before I continued, I asked them to try a problem. I wrote 48 on the board and explained, "I'd like each of you to use the process I've shown you to change 48 into a palindrome. I'll do it on the board as well. You can check your work with each other and against my work on the board." I did the problem:

$$\begin{array}{r} 48 \\ +\ 84 \\ \hline 132 \\ +\ 231 \\ \hline 363 \end{array}$$

The students understood the process, and all arrived at the same result once the few careless errors had been corrected. I then presented the exploration I wanted them to do.

PRESENTING THE INVESTIGATION

"You are to investigate all the numbers from 0 to 99. You'll be working together as a group, but you'll each record on the two sheets I've passed out. Let me explain how I want you to do this."

I held up the sheet with the numbers written in columns. "I'd like you to record the three numbers I did on the board first. I'll show you how." I introduced 13 first. "Find 13 on your sheet, in the first column. Because it took one step, write a 1 in the Steps column. And the resulting palindrome was 44, so write that in the Palindrome column." We did the same for 68 and 48.

I then focused them on the other sheet. "This sheet will give you a chance to examine visually the pattern of how many steps it takes to change numbers into palindromes. First you have to agree as a group on the colors you will use to color in numbers that are already palindromes, numbers that

* * * 0 - 99 CHART * * *

What colors are you using? Color in the small squares to show.

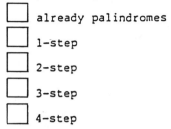

already palindromes

1-step

2-step

3-step

4-step

0	1	2	3	4	5	6	7	8	9
10	11	12	13	14	15	16	17	18	19
20	21	22	23	24	25	26	27	28	29
30	31	32	33	34	35	36	37	38	39
40	41	42	43	44	45	46	47	48	49
50	51	52	53	54	55	56	57	58	59
60	61	62	63	64	65	66	67	68	69
70	71	72	73	74	75	76	77	78	79
80	81	82	83	84	85	86	87	88	89
90	91	92	93	94	95	96	97	98	99

No.	Steps	Palindrome	No.	Steps	Palindrome	No.	Steps	Palindrome
10			40			70		
11			41			71		
12			42			72		
13			43			73		
14			44			74		
15			45			75		
16			46			76		
17			47			77		
18			48			78		
19			49			79		
20			50			80		
21			51			81		
22			52			82		
23			53			83		
24			54			84		
25			55			85		
26			56			86		
27			57			87		
28			58			88		
29			59			89		
30			60			90		
31			61			91		
32			62			92		
33			63			93		
34			64			94		
35			65			95		
36			66			96		
37			67			97		
38			68			98		
39			69			99		

take one step, two steps, and so on. Color in the small squares so you'll have a legend of your colors."

I asked for questions. So far there was none.

I continued with some procedural comments. "Decide as a group how you plan to work. I'll be asking you later how you divided up the work, if that method was a good one, and if you changed your method as you collected more information. Also, be sure you each complete the two record sheets."

I then concluded my introduction. "I have a few more comments before you begin to work. One is to look for patterns as you work. You may find that you don't have to do each number if you can use the information you're gathering along the way. I recommend that you color in as you work because you can get useful information from the chart as the pattern emerges. I'd like you to write summary statements about any patterns you find.

"And one caution. Beware of 89 and 98. Don't tackle those unless you are ready for a serious bout with addition. They require more addition than I think is reasonable, so do them at your own risk. I'll give answers for

Students eagerly work on the palindrome activity.

them on Friday. That gives you the week to struggle if you are interested, but it is not required." I wrote Beware of 89 and 98! on the board.

"Any questions before you get started?" I asked.

Kenny raised his hand. "Can we use our calculators?"

"Yes," I answered. It makes sense to allow students to use calculators when calculations are laborious. In this investigation the usefulness of the calculator runs out when sums exceed the number of digits in the display. Also, the students need to keep track of the number of addition steps each number takes; the calculator won't do that for them. This activity is a good one for helping students decide when and how a calculator is and is not useful.

Leah raised her question again, "What about the 0 through 9?"

"There are two ways to think about that. When you color in your 0–99 chart," I said, "you can see what would make sense to continue the pattern of colors. Also, if you were to make those two-digit numbers, you would have to put a 0 in the tens place for each number. Then 4 would become 04, even though we don't write it that way. That's another way to think about them. Talk about this in your groups."

Mark had a question. "How long do we have for this?" he asked.

"You won't be able to finish today, but you will make a start. Tomorrow just get back to work on it when it's time for math. Then you'll have to continue for homework or when you have free time during the day. I plan to summarize the activity on Friday, so you have the week to complete work on it." Having their own individual recording sheets made it possible for them to continue working on their own during the week.

DURING THE WEEK

The students dived right in, though the groups got organized in different ways. Deciding on the colors for the 0–99 chart was first on the agenda for several of the groups. The others were more interested in beginning with dividing up the work.

Groups shared the task in different ways. The strategy used by most of the groups was to divide up the numbers in some way they thought was fair. Two of the groups did it by using the 0–99 chart. One divided the chart into four quadrants, with each student taking one quadrant. Another divided it so each member had 2½ columns, so, they explained later, each would have some big and some small numbers.

Some groups used the other chart. Two divided the chart horizontally, thinking, as did the other group, that each should have larger and smaller numbers. In a group of three, each student took one column, and two of them figured that they'd have to help the person who had the column with the larger numbers. One group just divided up the numbers into four groups, 0–24, 25–49, 50–74, 75–99. All the groups seemed to decide to work individually, and then compile information after a while.

One group didn't divide up the numbers. They decided that each would work on different numbers and that for a while they would all record what they found on one of each sheet. They would look for patterns as they worked. Then when they were done, they would copy the work onto their individual records.

It was not initially obvious to any of the students that pairs of numbers with their digits reversed, 34 and 43, for example, would produce the same results. As groups made this discovery, they would rethink their method of dividing up the task so as to avoid duplication of efforts.

Also, the thought that larger numbers would require more work than smaller numbers had guided the dividing task for some of the groups. It soon emerged that this notion was false.

Half a dozen or so of the students were fascinated by 89 and 98 and were determined to see it to its conclusion. The first four that did so came up with varying results. Scott did it in seventeen steps, Lisa used twenty steps, and Mark and Steve both did it in twenty-four steps, though they each wound up with different resulting palindromes. This caused a good deal of buzzing in the class. I was glad that I had decided and announced that I would reveal the result on Friday. Though some pressured for the answer earlier, I resisted, giving them time to argue, compare, discuss. Giving the answer would merely stop their thinking and talking about the problem. I posted an additional notice: The answers to 89 and 98 will be revealed on Friday — and no sooner!

Most students abandoned their calculators fairly soon, finding them not very useful. Some were disappointed, feeling failed by the limits of the tool. This, too, was a useful lesson.

Students took great pleasure in having long columns of addition to look over and show each other. The quantity of their work seemed to make them feel extremely satisfied that they had accomplished a great deal. Probably as much adding practice went on that week as had been done so far the entire year.

DISCUSSING THE PATTERNS

Students discovered a variety of patterns, some from the 0–99 chart, some from the other chart, some from a combination of the two. Before beginning a class discussion of the activity on Friday, I gave groups time to gather their thoughts about patterns they had noticed and to write summary statements. Writing generalizations does not come easily to the students. However, this was not their first attempt, and their efforts showed improvement from former tries.

Most groups noticed the symmetry in the pattern they colored on the 0–99 chart. Though they didn't all use the word symmetry, they referred to the idea in their comments. "If you look at the numbers on the top and bottom of the line of already palindromes, the pattern is the same," Sara said. Scott added to that, "That's because every number has a reverse, like 64 and 46, and they're mirrors of themselves on the chart."

About the single-digit numbers, there was a general consensus that adding a zero in the tens place of each led to the conclusion that 0 was already a palindrome and 1 through 9 took one step in order to become palindromes.

Mark offered a different kind of pattern. "If the two numbers in a number add up to less than 10, then you know it will only take one step," he said.

"What do you mean by two numbers in a number?" I asked.

"You know, 23 has two numbers, 2 and 3," Mark explained.

"It's less confusing if you call them digits," I replied.

"Oh, yeah," Mark agreed. That was not a new word for him.

"How does the sum of the digits being less than 10 tell you that the number will take only one step to become a palindrome?" I pursued.

"Because there won't be any carrying then," Mark explained. "When there isn't any carrying, you get a palindrome."

"Yes," Jennifer added, "and the palindrome is always two of what the digits add up to."

"Can you give an example to illustrate that?" I asked Jennifer.

"Look at 34," she said, "the palindrome is 77, two 7s."

This cleared up her addition. Some of the other groups had also noticed these patterns. Others hadn't and were peering over their charts to check the conjectures.

Stephanie raised her hand to offer another pattern. "You can tell more from adding the digits," she said. Then she rattled off, "If they add to 10 or 12 or 13, they take two steps. If they add to 11, they take one step. If they add to 14, they take three steps. If they add to 15, they take four steps. If they add to 16, they take five steps."

"There's more," Steve said excitedly. "You always wind up with the same palindromes. All the numbers when the digits add to 10 or 11 always come up with 121. The ones that add to 12 come out 363. The ones that add to 13 come out to 484."

The class had gotten very noisy now, with groups who had not noticed these patterns looking over their work. With some difficulty I called the class back to order.

"It seems that some of you hadn't noticed these patterns yet," I told the class, "and I'll give you the chance in a moment to look for them. But first I have a question. Stephanie said that when the digits add to 10, the number takes two steps to become a palindrome, and Steve added that the palindrome will always be 121. What about the number 55?"

The class was quiet for a minute. Then Stephanie spoke, "I should have added 'except for 55.'"

"Let me write a complete sentence about what you know about numbers whose digits add to 10," I said. With the class I constructed a sentence: Except for 55, numbers whose digits add to 10 take two steps to become palindromes, and the palindrome is 121.

Modeling like this helps students develop the ability to write generalizations themselves.

Mark made a new discovery as we were talking. "I tried three-digit numbers, and it doesn't work," he said. "I tried 127 and 118. They only take one step and don't come out to 121. They each come out to different things."

"It seems that Mark has proved our sentence has a problem," I said. "How could we fix it?"

This was beyond some of the students' thinking.

Mark solved the problem. "Just start the sentence with 'For two-digit numbers' and it will be OK," he said.

I revised the sentence to read: For two-digit numbers, except for 55, numbers whose digits add to 10 take two steps to become palindromes, and the palindrome is 121.

At this point I gave the class some options to work on in their groups, sensing that their interests were varying. I brought the class back to attention and told them their choices.

"For those of you who haven't had a chance to investigate patterns such as Mark, Stephanie, and Steve have suggested, you may do that now and write what you find as summary statements. For others, you may want to look at patterns in three-digit numbers instead and see what summary statements you can write about them. And for those of you who feel you need a break from math, how about making a list of words that are palindromes. Here are some to get you started — mom, dad, wow, level, toot."

I listed their three choices on the board:

1. Write summary statements from the activity.
2. Write summary statements for three-digit numbers.
3. Look for words that are palindromes — mom, dad, wow, level, toot, etc.

They went to work for the rest of the class time.

Note: The numbers 89 and 98 take twenty-four steps. The resulting palindrome is 8,813,200,023,188.

WHAT NOW?

They say you understand something when you've taught it. I've always believed that. Nevertheless, I've become convinced from writing this book that you really understand something when you've written about it. I found that when writing the vignettes for this book, I had to examine all the teaching choices I have made. I had to interpret all the reactions I have received. I had to search for ways to communicate both what I was trying to do and why I was trying to do it. The thinking processes I needed to use in writing these vignettes contributed to my growth as a teacher, and for that I am grateful.

My goal in writing this book, however, was to contribute to your growth as well. I realize that fourteen lessons that span four grades certainly cannot in themselves make a substantive contribution to your math program. In that light the purpose of this book is not to provide a practical alternative to what you are now doing.

Instead, my goal is to offer you a vision of what I think math lessons ought to be—lessons in which children learn math through a problem-solving approach where their thinking and reasoning are valued and nurtured as they learn new mathematical concepts and skills. Though I hope that the specific suggestions offered by the lessons will serve you and your students, they do not in themselves have sustaining power. If the book is to have an effect, it will be from the principles underlying the lessons; they are the source of power.

For example, it is not the use of paper "cookies" that is the essence of the lesson on introducing fractions, but instead it is how the lesson models using a concrete material in a problem-solving situation to contribute to children's understanding. The week-long sequence on exploring multiplication through rectangles is important because it models teaching a topic basic to the curriculum in a problem-solving way that not only uses concrete materials, but that also helps students see different areas of mathematics in relation to each other. The lesson with the horse problem is not only a dynamic classroom opportunity, but also a demonstration of the importance of being able to reason as well as being able to do arithmetic computations.

My hope is that you'll approach this book with the same spirit of problem solving that the lessons promote. For starters, try the lessons. Even improve on them. Notice what you as a teacher learn about mathematics from them. Then examine the principles on which I built those classroom experiences by imagining the thinking I did when planning them. Finally, search for ways to incorporate these principles into your regular teaching. Remember, there is no one right way to do this, just as there is no one right way to approach solving a math problem.

INDEX